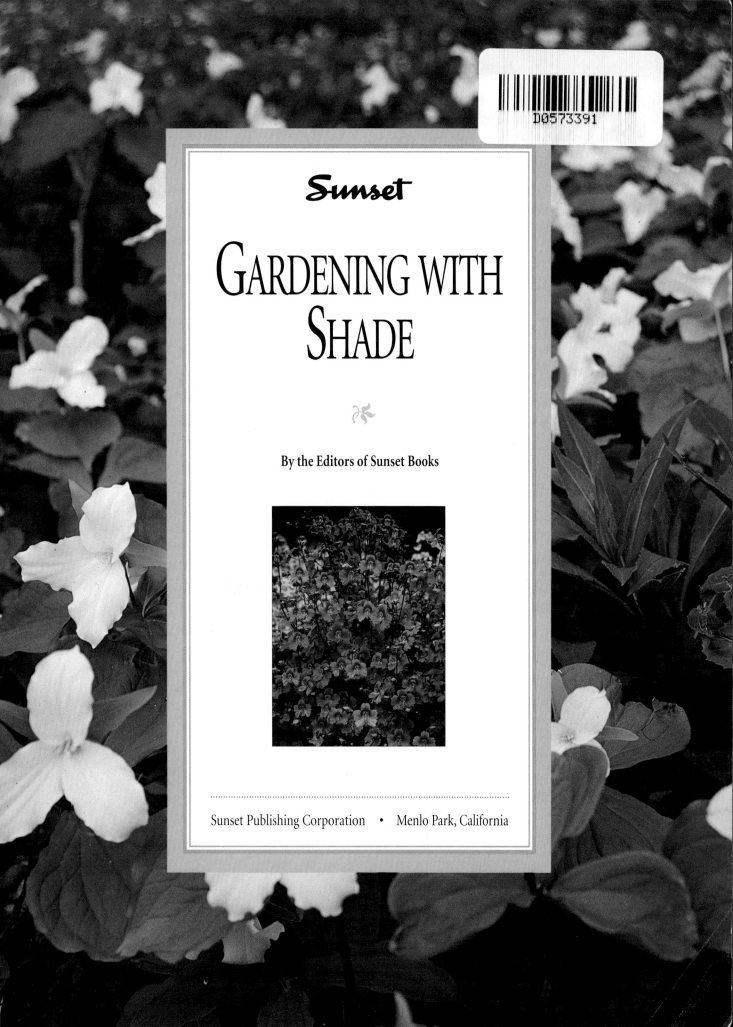

Sunset

GARDENING WITH SHADE

By the Editors of Sunset Books

Sunset Publishing Corporation • Menlo Park, California

Sunset
BOOKS

President & Publisher
Susan J. Maruyama

Director, Sales & Marketing
Richard A. Smeby

Director, New Business
Kenneth Winchester

Editorial Director
Bob Doyle

Marketing & Creative Services Manager
Guy C. Joy

Production Director
Lory Day

•

**EDITORIAL STAFF FOR
GARDENING WITH SHADE**

Coordinating Editor
Suzanne Normand Eyre

Research & Text
Philip Edinger

Design
Susan Sempere

Illustrations
Lois Lovejoy

Copy Editor
Phyllis Elving

Production Coordinator
Patricia S. Williams

•

SUNSET PUBLISHING CORPORATION

Chairman
Jim Nelson

President & Chief Executive Officer
Stephen J. Seabolt

Chief Financial Officer
James E. Mitchell

Publisher, Sunset Magazine
Anthony P. Glaves

Director of Finance
Larry Diamond

Circulation Director
Robert I. Gursha

Vice President, Manufacturing
Lorinda B. Reichert

Editor, Sunset Magazine
William R. Marken

•

First printing February 1996
Copyright © 1996 Sunset Publishing
Corporation, Menlo Park, CA 94025.
First edition. All rights reserved, including the
right of reproduction in whole or in any form.
ISBN 0-376-03846-2
Library of Congress Catalog Card: 95-72515
Printed in the United States.

•

If you would like to order additional copies of
any of our books, call us at 1-800-634-3095 or
check with your local bookstore. For special
sales, bulk orders, and premium sales information, call Sunset Custom Publishing &
Special Sales at (415) 324-5547.

SPOTLIGHT ON SHADE

*F*rom time immemorial, shade has provided cooling, refreshing refuge to humans. And yet, gardeners sometimes have regarded shade as an opponent—a gardening condition inhospitable to a number of favorite plants. In truth, there are countless fine (and favorite) plants that find shade just as inviting on a hot day as do we humans. The "secret" to shade gardening is really no secret at all. You have to match plants with the situation: learn the conditions shade imposes and the benefits it offers, then select plants from the great array that shun the sun.

The aim of this book is to put shade in the positive light it deserves, to reveal it as an opportunity. To be able to do this, we owe thanks to countless gardeners over the years who have experimented with shade gardening. They have been open to the possibilities of shade and have explored yet another aspect of the diverse world of horticulture. The result is that we may now compose shade gardens of great richness and subtle beauty.

Cover: Coleus, impatiens, and hosta provide a burst of color along a shady garden path. Landscape design: Charles Price and Glenn Withey. Cover design by Susan Bryant Caron. Photography by James Frederick Housel.

Title page: Trillium grandiflorum (outer photo) and Schizanthus pinnatus (inset).

Photographers:

Scott Atkinson: 26, 61 top right, 68 top; **Marion Brenner:** 58 left and bottom right, 83 bottom right; **Glenn Christiansen:** 37 top; **Crandall & Crandall:** 101 bottom; **Claire Curran:** 82 right, 90 right, 95 right; 96 left, 107 left, 110 left; **Alan Detrick:** 1 outer, 63 bottom right, 65 bottom right, 81 right, 108 left; **William B. Dewey:** 39 top; **Dick Dunmire:** 66 top right, 103 bottom right; **Derek Fell:** 64 bottom, 65 top right, 84 left, 85 right, 87 right, 95 middle, 99 top left, 105 left, 109 left; **Pamela Harper:** 77 bottom left; **Philip Harvey:** 39 bottom; **Saxon Holt:** 4, 12, 14 bottom, 18 left, 35 right, 47 left, 67, 71 top, 73 bottom left, 79 top, 83 top right, 87 left, 88 right, 91 right, 103 left; **Charles Mann:** 3 left, 8 top, 11 bottom, 15 bottom, 30 bottom, 31 bottom, 32 bottom, 41 right, 42 right, 45, 59 left, 63 left, 66 top left, 74 middle, 80 left, 88 left, 99 bottom left, 100, 106, 107 top right; **David McDonald:** 65 bottom left, 72 top left, 76 right, 77 top left, 86 right, 94 top, 99 right, 109 right; **Richard Nicol:** 13 top; **Don Normark:** 69 bottom; **Jerry Pavia:** 3 right, 10 top, 31 top, 33 top left and top right, 43 left, 49 middle, 51 middle, 53 left, 55 right, 56, 58 top right, 62 bottom left, 63 bottom middle, 71 bottom, 82 top left, 84 right, 85 middle, 93 right, 95 left, 101 top, 102, 105 right; **Joanne Pavia:** 11 top, 40, 77 right, 97 left; **Susan Roth:** 1 inset, 7 top left and top right, 8 bottom, 9 top, 10 bottom, 13 bottom, 29, 34, 46, 47 right, 50 left, 51 left and right, 52 right, 54 left and bottom right, 59 right, 60 bottom, 61 top and bottom left and top middle, 62 right, 65 top left, 66 bottom, 68 bottom, 72 bottom left, 73 top middle, 74 top left and bottom right, 75, 80 middle, 81 top left, 87 middle, 89 right, 91 left and middle, 92 top right, 94 bottom, 98 left, 107 bottom right, 110 right; **Michael S. Thompson:** 16, 30 top, 41 left, 42 left, 43 right, 44 right, 47 middle, 48, 49 left and right, 50 right, 55 left, 61 bottom right, 62 top left, 63 top right, 64 top, 69 top and middle, 70 bottom, 72 top right, 73 bottom middle and top right, 78, 79 bottom, 81 bottom left, 82 middle, 84 middle, 85 left, 89 left, 92 top left and bottom left, 96 right, 97 middle and right, 98 right, 103 top right, 104 left, 105 middle; **George Waters:** 90 left; **Russ Widstrand:** 18 top right, 23; **Doug Wilson:** 24 right, 104 right; **Cynthia Woodyard:** 7 bottom, 9 bottom, 14 top, 15 top, 20, 24 left, 25, 32 top, 33 bottom, 37 bottom, 44, 53 right, 54 top right, 70 top, 80 right, 83 left, 86 left, 92 bottom right, 93 left, 108 right; **Tom Wyatt:** 18 bottom right, 21, 35 left, 52 left, 60 top.

Contents

Thalictrum

Hosta and Astrantia

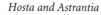

SHEDDING LIGHT ON SHADE

❧

*M*ention the word "shade" to anyone with a garden, and the word "problem" is a standard response. You hear about leggy, mildew-cloaked roses, irises that fail to flower, and annuals that— literally—never get off the ground. The implication is that gardening in the shade is a route strewn with failures and half-successes.   •   In reality, shade is a garden situation alive with possibilities. In these pages, you will meet shade in its various forms and discover that many plants actually prefer some degree of shade. And you'll be introduced to a wide world of shade plants from which you can compose gardens that will be the envy of your sun-gardening friends.

Dogwood trees (Cornus), flowers, and shade combine to present an enticing oasis of coolness and tranquility.

5

The Many Shades of Shade

All shade is not created equal. On a hot day, you may make no distinctions as you head for the nearest shady retreat. But plants do. While many "shade plants" have broad tolerances, there are limits to those tolerances. To put plants needing, say, the dappled sunlight of filtered shade alongside plants suited to deep shade is to court failure with one group or the other. The first step toward successful shade gardening, then, is to assess your shade. Study your garden throughout the year to note seasonal differences, too.

Geography plays a large part in determining the kind of shade you have. As you near the equator, the angle at which the sun strikes the earth is more direct; as you increase in latitude, the angle is more oblique. The more direct the rays, the more intense they are—so shade in the lower latitudes offers more contrast to sunlight in both light intensity and temperature. The angle of the sun's rays also affects shadow length: the more direct the rays, the shorter the shadow. Thus a one-story house in Mexico City will cast a smaller shadow than the same house in Toronto.

The longest shadows occur when the sun is at winter solstice: December in the northern hemisphere, June in the southern. The Mexico City house will cast its longest shadow of the year on December 21—but the Toronto house will cast a shadow that's even longer that day.

Camellia sasanqua

Geography determines climate in complex ways, and climate dictates the need for shade. In relatively cool-summer climates—often found both at higher latitudes and higher altitudes—shade is less needed as a refuge from sun. And where summer skies are overcast or foggy, as in many coastal regions, the sun's intensity is greatly toned down. In these situations, plants best suited for filtered, part, or open shade may succeed in locations that would be "full sun" when the sun was shining. And plants that would normally thrive in deep shade may prefer more light than a forest offers in such conditions.

After you have identified the conditions in your particular outdoor environment, you can make knowing choices from among the plants presented on pages 57–110. In the descriptions of these plants you will find the sort of shade each prefers—information directly linked to the types of shade discussed in the following pages.

Filtered Shade

Sunlight filters through a canopy of tree foliage, creating confetti-like patterns of light and shadow on plants and soil below. Not only does the pattern change from minute to minute as the sun progresses overhead from morning through afternoon, but it alters by the second as breezes stir the foliage.

This is classic dappled sunlight, typically called "filtered shade" even though it is sunlight rather than shade that is being filtered. The amount of light beneath the canopy depends on how dense the foliage is and how high the branching begins, but in all cases there is the play of sunlight and shadow. Often there will be enough light to satisfy some plants (such as daylilies) that also flourish in sunny beds. In general, filtered shade can support a great variety of shade plants—the options decreasing only as the shade becomes more dense. In all tree-shaded gardens, tree roots may be a factor, competing with plants for soil space, water, and nutrients (see page 24).

Even without trees, you can approximate open foliage by constructing an overhead structure of lath (see page 38). You sacrifice the constant changeability of light penetrating a moving canopy of leaves, but you do achieve a breakup of light that alters from minute to minute in the sun's daily progression through the sky.

Light filtering through trees—the patchwork shade of woods and forests—creates an atmosphere of coolness and calm.

•

Top left: *Woodland hostas luxuriate in filtered shade, their beauty reflected in a recreated woodland pond.*

Bottom left: *Dappled sunlight creates light-and-shadow play on white blossoms of evergreen azalea 'Glacier'.*

Top right: *A swarm of varied hostas and ferns are lighted, then shadowed, as the sun makes its daily transit.*

Bottom right: *Rustic bench invites contemplation of classic woodland fern garden.*

Part Shade

Every homeowner knows the partly shaded garden. During the morning hours, shade bathes the land on the west side of the house, the shaded territory decreasing as the sun rises in the sky. Conversely, the ground on the east side of the house becomes increasingly shaded as the afternoon advances.

That is "part shade" in its simplest form. In the garden, this kind of shade can also be created by fences and walls, other structures, and plantings. A high hedge or small tree to the east of the house, for example, may intercept early morning sun—thus reducing the number of hours sunlight strikes the ground.

In partly shaded gardens where the source of greatest light always is from one direction, many plants will "face the light": their strongest growth will occur on the side toward the light, and flower stems will lean that way. Whenever possible, arrange part-shade plantings so they will be viewed from the "sunny" side.

Remember that shadow patterns will vary according to the time of year and the sun's elevation in the sky as well as your latitude (see page 6).

Aquilegia hybrid

❧

*A brief, daily "sunshine fix" sustains
many plants through shady
hours to follow.*

•

Top left: *Daylilies (Hemerocallis) and astilbe
mount a winning performance with
only morning sunlight.*

Bottom left: *Mixed daylilies and
hostas face the morning sun.*

Top right: *Just a few hours of
daily sun bring on lavish blossoming of
'Irene Koster' deciduous azalea
and Endymion hispanicus.*

Bottom right: *Hydrangea macrophylla and
massive Hosta sieboldiana retreat into
afternoon shade as sun disappears
behind stone wall.*

Open Shade

What characterizes open shade is the absence of overhead obstruction to sunlight. This comes about in several ways. Urban gardeners know open shade well: many city garden plots are always in the shadow of multistory buildings despite being completely open to the sky. In the suburbs or even the country, tall trees may cast shadow over a garden for half of the day, while structural walls take over the shade-casting for the other half.

Open shade frequently is well lighted even though direct sunlight is not a part of the equation. Plants that prefer filtered shade and partial shade usually find congenial light quality in open shade. Even though there is no direct sunlight, plants growing near buildings and walls will tend to concentrate their growth on the sides facing away from the wall, just as plants in partial shade will face the light.

To create a lightly shady sanctuary for plants and people where it doesn't occur naturally, you can adapt the methods used by commercial shade plant growers to gain ground for their stock. A post-and-beam structure will support an overhead of shade cloth that will evenly diffuse sunlight to a precise degree of shadiness, depending on the weave of cloth you choose. See page 38 for overhead structure ideas.

Mahonia aquifolium

Deep Shade

The name says it all. Step into this kind of shade on a sunny day, and you have to pause to let your eyes adjust. Because the level of light is so low compared to other shady situations, this is the most restrictive kind of shade when it comes to choosing plants.

In nature, you find deep shade in dense forests. In gardens, deep shade exists under large trees, particularly evergreens that have thick canopies and branch fairly low to the ground. But it also occurs where not a tree is in sight—in a narrow side yard to the north of a house, for example, especially where a neighboring house or adjacent fence blocks light. A recessed entryway, with planting beds snuggled into the corners, is likely to offer nothing but deep shade—particularly if it faces north. The same can be said of the ground-floor recessed patio in a multistory housing unit.

Fatsia japonica

Seasonal shade takes two opposite forms. One is the plot of land shaded in winter by buildings or evergreen trees that intercept the sun at its lowest angle of the year. As the year progresses and the sun's path rises, the ground becomes increasingly less shaded until, by mid- to late spring, it is in full sun. This land can support a wide assortment of sun-loving plants.

The shade gardener may encounter the opposite situation beneath or adjacent to deciduous trees. From autumn until spring, sunlight reaches the ground through bare limbs. But from the moment trees leaf out until they lose their leaves the next autumn, the ground is shaded. This creates a perfect home for certain winter- and early spring-flowering bulbs and perennials that need sun from the onset of growth through flowering but then prefer shade or become dormant. This also can be home to shade-loving deciduous perennials and shrubs—plants that have leafy (and flowery) growth only from spring through early autumn, when shade is provided from above.

❧

Sun in winter, shade in summer is a comfortable alternation for many plants as well as people.

•

Above: Bare limbs of deciduous trees and shrubs barely obstruct sunlight for winter-blooming Crocus tomasinianus and Eranthis hyemalis.

Right: Lenten rose (Helleborus orientalis) reveals its varied blossoms to the winter sun, but plants need the protection of shade in the warmer months.

WORKING
WITH SHADE

Look upon shade and gardening as a partnership.

While shade does establish a set of conditions, it

also offers opportunities not available in a sunny

patch. And since basic gardening techniques are the

same in any exposure, there is no new set of "rules"

to learn. • In the following eight pages, you'll

become acquainted with the conditions shade

imposes on familiar gardening procedures such as

soil preparation and watering. You'll learn how to

have a successful lawn in shade. And you'll find

that there are ways to overcome two potential

problems: shade that increases as trees grow larger,

and encroaching tree roots.

Springtime floral fireworks illuminate this part- and
open-shade landscape, designed specifically for
maximum color impact.

Soil & Water

Even though shade imposes its own particular conditions on plant selection and gardening practices, a successful shade garden still begins where any successful garden does. It is built on a foundation of soil and water. Understanding what this means for your own garden situation will get you off to the right start.

Improving Your Soil

Gardeners speak of the extremes of "heavy" and "light" soils and that ideal gardening soil—"loam." All of them, despite differences in their properties, are complex compositions of mineral material (the soil particles), organic matter, water, air, and micro-organisms. Soil type is determined by the mineral materials; its quality is influenced by the other ingredients.

Clay soils are composed of tiny, flattened mineral particles that pack together almost like cards in a deck. Such dense or "heavy" soils have little space between particles for water to enter, so water penetration is slow; these soils are known as "poorly drained." Gluelike when wet, they're like concrete when dry.

Sandy soils, on the other hand, are composed of relatively large, irregularly rounded particles that fit together rather like beans in a jar. Compared to clay, these soils are "light." Spaces between particles are large enough to let water pass freely, resulting in a "well-drained" soil. When wet, sandy soil is gritty and damp; when dry, it is dusty.

Loam is not a soil type (in soil science parlance) but more of a condition. A loam soil contains a mix of particle sizes as well as organic matter. This is perfect "vegetable gardening" soil—moisture-

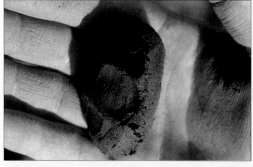

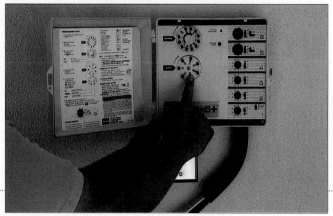

retentive but not soggy, with organic matter to keep it in top condition.

Organic additions. Organic matter is the key to improving soil. In clay soils, it lodges between particles and particle aggregates, opening up the soil so water can pass through more freely. In sandy soil, it literally fills in some of the pore spaces, acting rather like a sponge to slow the passage of water. Micro-organisms continually work at breaking down organic matter; this releases small amounts of nutrients, but more importantly it produces humus, a gel-like substance that binds small particles into larger aggregates to produce soil that is easy to dig and easy for roots to penetrate.

For the shade gardener, organic matter can hardly be overemphasized. Many shade plants are native forest dwellers, accustomed to a soil constantly supplemented by nature's compost of fallen leaves decomposing to produce a porous, organically rich soil. To approximate this forest soil, you can choose from a wide range of organic materials—traditional homemade compost, purchased nitrogen-stabilized wood by-products, peat moss, mushroom compost, animal manures, and a variety of regionally available agricultural by-products.

Watering in the Shade

The plant descriptions in the "Encyclopedia of Shade Plants" beginning on page 57 include the moisture needs for each plant. Some plants are noted as preferring plenty of moisture, even the nearly saturated soil at the edge of a pond. At the opposite extreme, a few are quite drought-tolerant—accustomed to soil that dries considerably between applications of water. The majority of shade plants, though, need fairly regular watering for best performance—the sort of watering you'd give a vegetable garden or a planting of annuals.

In shade, however, "regular watering" may call for a different schedule. Without sunshine and heat to cause evaporation, soil in shade is likely to stay moist longer than soil in sun. What prevents this statement from being absolute is the variable of roots. Trees shading a garden may have extensive root systems, and trees with networks of roots near the surface can absorb so much moisture that you'll be compelled to water on a "sunny garden" schedule.

General guidelines for watering remain the same for shade gardens as for sunny ones. Water long enough so that water will penetrate deeply. It is true that "shallow watering leads to shallow roots"—and shallow-rooted plants are the first to suffer when the soil begins to dry. Remember that water penetrates clay soils—even those amended with organic matter—more slowly that sandy soils. Adjust your watering time to the type of soil you have.

❧

Far left: All good gardens stem from an understanding of the soil. And rare is the soil that won't benefit from some improvement, even if it's nothing more elaborate than digging.

Near left, top: Dense clay soil—commonly called "heavy"—forms a solid, unbreakable mass if squeezed when moist.

Near left, bottom: An electronic controller can take charge of your garden watering. This multiprogram model will handle diverse water needs, turning systems on and off according to your directions.

The Lawn in Shade

What could be lovelier than a patch of cool, velvety lawn spreading a verdant invitation to enter the shade garden? The image is alluring; too often, though, the grassy carpet materializes threadbare and moth-eaten. But shade doesn't mean you have to accept second-rate turf. Advance planning will put you on the path to success.

To achieve a good lawn, whether in shade or sun, you must follow these three guidelines: prepare the soil well (see the Sunset book *Lawns* for guidelines); choose grasses appropriate for your climate and situation; and follow a consistent maintenance program. For shade gardening, the second point is critical; without the right grasses, your efforts will be wasted.

The Right Grass for You

Lawn grasses divide into two categories. Cool-season grasses withstand cold winters but do poorly where summers are hot—especially if they're both hot and dry. Warm-season grasses, on the other hand, grow lustily where it's warm to hot in summer, but most are subtropical in origin and won't survive cold winters.

And nearly all warm-season kinds become brown as they go dormant over winter.

The best choices for shady lawns are cool-season grasses that thrive in the Pacific Northwest, the northern California coast, the Rocky Mountain states, the northern Midwest, and the Northeast. Prominent among these are several fescues (Chewings, creeping red, and hard) and rough-stalk bluegrass. Moderately successful in shade are Colonial bent grass, Kentucky bluegrass, and tall fescue.

Among warm-season grasses suited to mild-winter regions in the Southeast, South, and Southwest, only St. Augustine grass truly flourishes in shade. But it is a rampantly spreading, course-textured grass that is far from golf course quality.

❧

Above: As good as a putting green, this velvety turf results from thoughtful choice of grass and meticulous maintenance.

Left: Shifting shadows cast by mature deciduous oak trees play across a manicured meadow of a lawn.

Moderate successes in shade among warm-season types are Bahia grass (course-textured); centipede grass and seashore paspalum (medium-textured); and fine-textured zoysia.

In the transitional zones of the lower Midwest and upper South—where summer is hot but winter sometimes too harsh for some warm-season grasses—you'll find shade successes in both camps. Among the cool-season types, rough-stalk bluegrass, Kentucky bluegrass, and tall fescue are used. Zoysia is the best warm-season turf choice, followed by centipede grass.

For central and western plains states, characterized by hot summers and cold winters, latitude is the deciding factor. In northern regions, choose the fescues and bluegrasses. In more southerly territory, grow tall fescue or perhaps zoysia.

Plain or Mixed?

Grass seed is sold in two ways: as individual grass or as a blend of several kinds. A lawn composed of a single grass will be the most uniform in appearance, but if it becomes victim to a particular pest, disease, or environmental condition (such as unusual heat or drought), the entire turf will be at risk.

A blend of grasses minimizes the disaster risk—the grasses that persist will be those that do best in your climate, soil, situation, and maintenance regime. Grass seed producers offer packaged "shade mixtures"; check the labels for names of grasses they include to see if they are suited to your climate.

❧ LAWN GRASSES ❧

Creeping red fescue

Chewings fescue

Hard fescue

Rough-stalk bluegrass

Zoysia

Centipede grass

Pruning to Let in the Light

Tree-shaded gardens have a habit of becoming shadier over time, and this can lead to a decline in performance by plants that originally thrived. Two factors account for this. First, as trees grow taller they cast longer and longer arms of shade. And second, tree canopies become more complex as a tree grows, and less light can penetrate an increasingly solid leaf cover.

There's little you can do to limit a tree's height. Topping is not recommended: the result is aesthetically unpleasing, and many trees will try to repair the damage by sending new growth upward into the formerly occupied space. This obligates you to repeated bouts of ugliness and renewal.

There are, however, two pruning approaches that will admit more light to a tree-shaded garden without compromising the beauty of the trees.

Canopy Raising

The quickest way to admit more light under trees is to remove lower limbs—raising the foliage canopy so that more light from the sides, even a bit of sunlight, will be available in mornings and afternoons. This is simplest with whorl-branching conifers (such as pines), since the removal of just one set of limbs can make a significant difference. With randomly-branched trees, you'll need to carefully consider what lower-limb removal will do to the overall tree shape.

Canopy Thinning

In this process, you selectively remove branches from within the tree's canopy, letting more light reach the ground beneath. Sometimes removing two or three limbs will make a significant difference; in other cases, you can achieve the desired result by selectively removing countless smaller branches throughout the entire canopy (see photos on facing page). You control the result by determining how much material will be thinned from the tree. In time, you'll need to repeat the process as trees grow larger and fill in the gaps.

Canopy thinning is a process that requires careful thought and skilled work—preferably by a licensed professional who has the proper experience, tools, and insurance.

Pruning Shrubs

You can use the same techniques of canopy raising and thinning on large, shade-casting shrubs, too. By removing lower limbs, large shrubs will instantly become shrub-trees, as shown at left, with considerably more light reaching the

Pruning can transform a bulky mature shrub into a small tree. Select major stems to become trunks, then remove lower branches to the desired canopy height.

ground beneath their newly-created canopies. By simply thinning a high and dense hedge, you can create a light-permeable screen that leaves a more congenial growing space on its shady side.

❧

By thinning out a tree's branches, you can decrease the density of shade beneath its canopy.

·

Before thinning, top: Vigorous deciduous tree has produced so many branches, stems, and twigs that the summertime foliage canopy obscures all light.

During thinning, middle: Major limbs are well placed, creating an evenly balanced head, so no major limb removal is needed. The first growth to be removed consists of the smallest-diameter, twiggy stems within the tree's center.

After thinning, bottom: The finished product shows a much more open center, with considerably more space between remaining branches. The outer branches were also cut back to produce a symmetrically rounded canopy outline.

Dealing with Root Competition

Where you have large shade trees, you also have the root systems that support them. Some trees are agreeably deep-rooted, leaving the upper reaches of the soil relatively free for root growth of smaller plants. Other trees—including some of the best shade-casters, such as maples—spread out their roots close enough to the surface to pose real competition to other plantings.

These shallow root systems insinuate themselves through the soil, making it difficult to dig soil, amend it, and set out other plants. They also take the lion's

Hanging basket overflowing with colorful shade plants artfully dodges tree-root competition.

share of moisture and nutrients, starving the lesser plants within their reach. What to do?

Some Solutions

The most laborious solution—and not a permanent one—is to root prune the tree by digging a trench approximately 18 inches wide and deep in a circle around the tree at the edge of its foliage canopy, then removing roots and returning the soil to the trench. For extra insurance, you can install a metal or a poured concrete barrier in the trench before refilling

it. Sooner or later, however, roots will grow back through the root-free zone and may even work their way beneath any barrier to come up on the "safe" side. And, of course, any plantings beneath the tree's branches still are subject to competition from its roots.

A select few shrubs and perennials have the ability to succeed in the root-infested soil of larger trees. Planting them is a pragmatic solution to the problem—if you're willing to settle for a limited plant choice. But there are easier ways to work around the obstacle.

Containing the problem. The most practical solution to tree-root competition—one that gives the soil to the trees yet leaves you with a wide plant choice—is to turn to container gardening. From clay pots to ambitious planter beds, the principle is the same: soil is contained, keeping it free from outside competition. For a list of good container plants to grow in shaded gardens, see page 45.

Container gardening offers several benefits. One is that you can give individual care to each container, watering and fertilizing for optimum plant perfor-

mance. In containers, you can even succeed with plants unsuited to growing in the ground in the soil of your garden. Since you can move any container not firmly connected to its spot (such as planters and window boxes), you can shift plants if they need more or less shade. And you can move your containers around, rearranging them when you want a new look and rotating plants so that the display is always attractive. A wood deck or patio surface of brick or stone will create an outdoor-living surface that lets water reach tree roots in the soil beneath.

❧

Far left: A tree-shaded white garden relies on containers and raised beds to present its floral displays of cyclamen, hydrangeas, impatiens, and nicotiana.

Near left: Containerized cornucopias of summer color crown this patio with showy impatiens and fuchsias trained into tree form.

Right: One window box can become an eye-level minigarden, as demonstrated by this thriving Serbian bellflower (Campanula poscharskyana).

PLANNING YOUR SHADE GARDEN

Chances are you won't need to decide where to put a shade garden—just what to do with the shady patch you have. In shade, as you'll see in the following pages, certain design principles take on added importance. You'll also see how water can be used as a tantalizing "extra." And you'll even learn how to create more shade without waiting for a tree to grow.   •   To simplify the planning process, we've grouped shade plants into categories to help you meet your design needs. Use the charts on the following pages in conjunction with the plant encyclopedia on pages 57–110.

This meticulously-groomed garden shows that elegance is attainable in shade, given the proper plants and good design.

27

Designing with Shade

Finding a broad assortment of plants that will thrive in the shade is not difficult; the "Encyclopedia of Shade Plants" on pages 57–110 proves the point. The greater challenge lies in designing a shade garden with an assemblage of plants that makes a visually distinct picture.

In a sunny garden, it's easy to catch the eye—colorful flowers do the trick. But in the reduced light of shaded gardens, visibility is less assured. Unless you give advance thought to the plants you choose and where you put them, you may achieve a horticultural triumph but visually produce only a pointillist blur of green dots and shadows.

Color for Accent

Light colors reflect light, while dark colors absorb it. In the reduced light of the shade garden, therefore, lighter-colored blossoms will sparkle, leaving violet, maroon, bronze, and indigo receding into the foliage.

That doesn't mean you have to forsake the less flashy hues. Such subtly-colored plants as *Iris foetidissima* (Gladwin iris) and *Tricyrtis hirta* (toad lily) can be successes in your shade garden if you place them where they can be appreciated at close range—next to a garden bench, for example.

Despite the range of flowering plants suitable for shade, the prevailing color in a shaded garden

is green. To alleviate the all-green look, use a generous mixture of plants with variegated or non-green leaves. These will contribute the same sort of sparkle as light-colored flowers—with the additional advantage of offering it from spring through autumn or even, in the case of evergreens, all year long.

Hostas probably offer the greatest assortment of variegated-leaf selections as well as plants with foliage in chartreuse, nearly yellow, frosty gray, and virtually blue. But many other perennials and shrubs also have foliage variants with yellow, cream, or white markings. Liberally distributed among entirely green-leafed plants, the variegated- and colored-leaf individuals will help highlight the all-green members of the landscape as well as call attention to themselves.

Lamium maculatum
'Beacon Silver'

Light, bright, and white colors—and foliage that is more than just green—will enliven any shade planting.

•

Top: *Pristine whiteness of impatiens stands out against intricate foliage pattern of five-finger fern (Adiantum aleuticum).*

Center right: *A snowdrift of white azaleas relieves the shadowiness of this basically green landscape.*

Center left: *A profusion of azaleas in bright red and white calls attention to color, leaving the green boxwood and liriope as soft framework for the composition.*

Bottom: *With the structure furnishing a color note, only a mass planting of white is needed to further illuminate the shade.*

Introducing Texture

The shadow patterns and reduced light in shady gardens can mute distinctions between plants. If you have a grouping of half a dozen different plants with similar foliage, the visual impression is more likely to be of a single "blob" than of individual plants.

A good way to avoid this problem is to juxtapose plants with different leaf sizes and shapes. Consider the possibilities: the grasslike foliage of various grasses and daylilies; the boat-shaped foliage of hostas and aspidistra; and the great leafy fans and paddles of *Fatsia japonica* (Japanese aralia) and *Bergenia*. This is just a sampling of the diversity of leaf shapes available for you to "arrange" in your garden.

Even among the many plants that have more-or-less oval leaves, these leaves range in size from the tiny presentations of boxwood and barberry plants to real "statements" among some hydrangeas and rhododendrons.

When you add flowers to the pool of textural possibilities, the potential for contrast increases further. Remember, though, that flowers appear as momentary accents against the more constant backdrop of foliage.

Helleborus niger

Large versus small, intricate versus uncomplicated, circular versus linear—these are the sorts of leaf and flower texture contrasts that will stand out distinctly in a shadowy garden.

•

Top left: Bold, bell-like rhododendron blossoms and the egg-shaped tulip find their textural opposite in the filagree fineness of fern foliage.

Bottom left: Effective combination of textures and colors features oak-leaf hydrangea, a variegated hosta, purple-leaf Japanese barberry, and a dwarf pine.

Above: Bold, broad-leafed hosta and demure, fine-textured astrantia present a picture of simplicity in opposites.

Right: Even among large-leafed plants, you can achieve effective contrast in shapes. Here, a maple-leafed Viburnum opulus shares the shade with the lilypad-like leaves of Hosta sieboldiana elegans.

Plant Size & Shape

Contrasting sizes works on two levels to further create texture in your shade garden. First, you can combine large- and small-leafed plants to highlight both. A small-leafed background will focus attention on the large-leafed plant in front of it; bold foliage in the rear, on the other hand, makes the eye focus both on that plant and on the fine-textured foliage in the foreground.

The second way to capitalize on size difference is to combine plants of conspicuously differing height and bulk. A low shrub backed by a medium-tall one may register as a green lump, but the same low shrub will stand out when planted in front of a small tree. To illustrate the point, visualize the airy grace of columbine *(Aquilegia)* displayed against a solid, substantial wall of camellia foliage—or a fountain of daylily leaves partially concealing the bare lower limbs of a witch hazel shrub *(Hamamelis)*.

By combining plants of different growth habits, you achieve contrasts that spotlight individual plants, visually separating them from one another. Rather than grouping plants that are all rounded and mounding, for instance, try planning dynamic combinations that include vertical shapes, spreading ones, fountains of foliage, and the shuttlecock form typical of many ferns.

❧

Textural contrast alone will make an interestingly varied planting. Add to that the contrasts of sizes and shapes and the planting becomes truly dynamic.

•

Top left: *Fountains of daylilies, nosegays of bergenia, and a sea of forget-me-nots exhibit strong contrasts in size, shape, and texture.*

Bottom left: *The composition is vertical, but tall and large foxgloves tower over the smaller candelabra primroses in the foreground.*

Above: *Besides contrasts in texture, this grouping includes three different shapes—upright astilbe, a shuttlecock-shape fern, and rounded Euonymus fortunei 'Silver Queen'.*

Top right: *This grouping includes small (Endymion hispanicus), medium (Hosta fortunei 'Aurea'), and large plants (yellow deciduous azalea), yet the hosta makes the dominant size statement.*

Bottom right: *Simple planting of Woodwardia fern and sweet woodruff ground cover derives its effectiveness from the extreme differences in size and shape.*

Using Water in Shade

Shade and water are a natural combination, both suggesting coolness and refreshment. What could be more appropriate than incorporating a spot of water into your shade garden plans?

Your watery options run from the miniature to the grandiose; the only limiting factors are your space and your budget. All you really need is water and some sort of vessel to contain it.

Sometimes the simplest statement is the most effective: a shallow, fern-enfringed pond, sunk into a woodland opening; or a no-frills birdbath elevated on a pedestal above a rippling sea of hosta foliage.

At the other end of the scale are grottoed waterfalls propelled by recirculating pumps, the outflow streaming through the landscape or contained in one or more mirrorlike ponds. Here the shady landscape can be formed around the water feature, rather than the water serving as a minor accent in the overall scheme.

Let the design of your water feature reflect the setting—formal or naturalistic, as befits your garden. For detailed how-to information on using water in your garden, consult the Sunset book *Garden Pools, Fountains & Waterfalls.*

Acer palmatum 'Atropurpureum'

❧

*Shaded gardens are a natural home to the
soothing sight and sound of water.*

·

Far left, top: *A simple bird bath is embraced by Astilbe
'Avalanche', filmy Miscanthus sinensis, and a
lacy Dryopteris fern.*

Far left, bottom: *A sunken pond is framed by the leafy
greenness of hostas and ferns, while columbines and
primroses add sparks of color.*

Above: *Delicate Japanese maple foliage
contrasts with this rugged, Japanese-style water feature.*

Near left: *Vigorously moving water courses through a
naturalistic setting prominently planted with
pachysandra, liriope, and ferns.*

Adding Shade with Vines & Structures

Sometimes you may want to create shade where none exists. You needn't rely on trees alone to supply shade. Vigorous vines trained on overhead supports can filter or block the sunlight to the satisfaction of both plant and human shade-seekers. Or you can achieve instant shade by fabricating overhead structures that will filter or block sunlight to just the degree you want.

Vines for Shade

You'll find vines profiled in the "Encyclopedia of Shade Plants," pages 57–110, that not only prosper in the shade but also can grow in sunshine and cast shade. These include *Akebia quinata*, *Ampelopsis brevipedunculata*, some of the *Clematis* species, the larger-growing *Lonicera* species, *Parthenocissus quinquefolia*, and *Trachelospermum jasminoides*.

Numerous vines that thrive in sunshine might be planted to cast shade. Some of the most popular, with the greatest visual appeal, are presented here.

Deciduous vines. Among sun-loving vines that lose their leaves in autumn, *Wisteria* is a favorite. Its rapid, vigorous, twining growth will cover an arbor with attractive foliage. In early spring, before leaves emerge, long clusters of flowers shaped like sweet peas mount a breathtaking display. Chinese wisteria, *W. sinensis*, is the most common, offering flowers in lavender, violet, pink, and white. Japanese wisteria, *W. floribunda*, has flowers in the same colors, but in longer clusters. Both are hardy to –20°F/–29°C.

A number of climbing roses can furnish color and shade; consult specialist catalogs for choices. Lady Banks' rose, *Rosa banksiae*, is a favorite in the mild-winter areas of the South, Southwest, and West; its flowers are the size of a quarter but smotheringly abundant in spring—yellow or white, single or double. Another mild-climate favorite is 'Mermaid', which produces large, single yellow blossoms throughout the year against a far-reaching backdrop of glossy leaves. In colder regions, choice is restricted to roses developed from hardy species. Single, carmine pink 'American Pillar' is an old favorite, reliable to –20°F/–29°C.

Trumpet creepers (*Campsis* species) will take winter temperatures to –20°F/–29°C. Their vigorous stems attach to vertical surfaces by means of aerial rootlets. Common trumpet creeper, *C. radicans*, produces summer clusters of trumpet-shaped orange and red blossoms. The hybrid *C. × tagliabuana* 'Mme. Galen' has trumpet-flowers of salmon red.

Exuberant vines can make leafy umbrellas of shade when given an expansive overhead structure for support. These deciduous vines give shade during the warmest months but admit sunlight during their leafless winter period.

•

Above: *Clusters of Japanese wisteria blossoms hang like elegant stalactites through an overhead structure of wooden beams.*

Left: *A thriving grape vine knows no bounds, easily covering a rustic overhead with bold foliage and perhaps even tasty fruits.*

If you want fruit rather than flowers, look to grapes for good shade. The vines are sturdy and structurally interesting, outfitted in bold foliage that colors well in autumn. There are numerous named varieties of both wine grapes and table grapes. To learn which are the best fruiting varieties for your area, consult your county or state agricultural extension service.

Evergreen vines. Where winter low temperatures reliably remain above 20°F/–7°C, the shading-vine possibilities expand considerably.

Several vines offer trumpet-shaped flowers in various colors; all climb by means of tendrils. Violet trumpet vine, *Clytostoma callistegioides,* produces large, pale violet flowers from late spring to autumn on a vigorous, easy-to-grow plant. Blossoms of blood red trumpet vine, *Distictis buccinatoria,* open orange-red but fade to bluish red; bloom comes in cycles throughout the year. Yellow trumpet vine, *Macfadyena unguis-cati,* flowers in early spring against a setting of glossy leaves.

Where frost is rare or light, nothing is more spectacular than *Bougainvillea.* For much of the year, its vines produce showers of brilliant blossomlike bracts in tropically vivid colors—violet, cerise, hot pink, red, orange, yellow—as well as warm bronze tones. The plant's thorny stems must be tied in place.

Trachelospermum jasminoides

For summer fragrance, two jasmines offer clustered white blossoms on twining vines with fine-textured foliage. *Jasminum officinale* grows to 30 feet; half that size is *J. grandiflorum.*

Giant Burmese honeysuckle, *Lonicera hildebrandiana,* is a greatly magnified version of familiar honeysuckle vines. Ropelike, twining stems bear hand-sized leaves and 7-inch summer flowers that open white, then turn yellow to orange.

Overhead Structures

When you need to add an oasis of shade to a sun-soaked garden, constructing an overhead sunscreen is the fastest way to get results. Your shade structure might be freestanding in a special spot in the garden, or it might be attached to the house in order to shade both the ground and the house wall.

Overhead support for vines may be simple post-and-beam construction with enough additional horizontal members to support vine growth. But with a few more materials, you can fashion an attractive arbor, pergola, or overhead that will cast shade by itself. Imagination and observation will suggest numerous design possibilities and materials combinations.

A simple box frame held aloft by four posts can be customized by your choice of overhead materials. The classic lathhouse, for example, is roofed over by lath strips spaced an inch or so apart so that light can penetrate. A more substantial version could employ 2-by-2s, 2-by-4s, or other dimensioned lumber to create the light-and-shade patterns.

To establish uniform shade, you can also stretch commercial shade cloth over a simple framework. Shade cloth is available from hardware and building supply stores in several weaves, allowing for greater or lesser light penetration. Even natural canvas will let light through while blocking the sun's direct rays.

Where winter low temperatures are not a limiting factor, many vigorous evergreen vines can give longed-for shade in short order. Many of them offer a summerlong show of colorful blossoms.

•

Above: In an explosion of color, bougainvillea vines offer a tropical extravaganza wherever frost is light or absent. The wide color assortment available lets you mix colors in imaginative combinations.

Right: Climbing roses have a universal appeal, and the available choices include fairly cold-hardy plants as well as those suited just to mild-winter climates.

Flower Color for Shade

DAPHNE × burkwoodii

Nothing lightens up shade more than color. Fortunately, there is a wide choice of colorful flowers with which to decorate a shade scene. For additional possibilities, see "Annuals" (page 60) and "Bulbs" (page 63).

		TYPE/ HARDINESS	FLOWER COLOR
ABUTILON Flowering maple	p. 58	Evergreen shrubs/ 25°F/–4°C	White, yellow, orange, pink, red
ACANTHUS mollis Acanthus, bear's breech	p. 58	Evergreen perennial/ 0°F/–18°C	Purple and white
ACONITUM Aconite, monkshood	p. 59	Deciduous perennials/ –30°F/–34°C	White, pink, violet, blue
AJUGA reptans Ajuga, carpet bugle	p. 62	Evergreen perennial ground cover/ –30°F/–34°C	Blue
ALCHEMILLA mollis Lady's mantle	p. 62	Deciduous to semi-evergreen perennial/ –40°F/—40°C	Yellow-green
ANEMONE × hybrida Japanese anemone	p. 63	Semideciduous perennial/ –20°F/–29°C	White, pink
AQUILEGIA Columbine	p. 63	Deciduous perennials/ –35°F/–37°C (species), –20°F/–29°C (hybrids)	White, yellow, pink, red, purple, blue
ARBUTUS unedo Strawberry tree	p. 64	Evergreen tree, shrub/ 5°F/–15°C	White, pink
ARUNCUS dioicus Goatsbeard	p. 64	Deciduous perennials/ –35°F/–37°C	Cream
ASTILBE Astilbe, false spiraea, meadow sweet	p. 65	Deciduous perennials/ –25°F/–32°C	White, pink, red, magenta
ASTRANTIA Masterwort	p. 66	Deciduous perennials/ –10°F/–23°C	White, pink
AZARA Azara	p. 66	Evergreen shrubs/ Varies	Yellow
BEGONIA × tuberhybrida Tuberous begonia	p. 68	Deciduous tuberous perennial/ Tender	White, cream, yellow, orange, pink, red
BERBERIS Barberry	p. 68	Deciduous and evergreen shrubs/ Varies	Yellow
BERGENIA Bergenia	p. 69	Deciduous and evergreen perennials/ Varies	White, pink, rosy purple, magenta
BLETILLA striata Chinese ground orchid	p. 69	Deciduous perennial/ 10°F/–12°C	White, lavender

		TYPE/ HARDINESS	FLOWER COLOR
BRUNNERA macrophylla Brunnera, Siberian bugloss	p. 69	Deciduous perennial/ –35°F/–37°C	Blue
CAMELLIA Camellia	p. 71	Evergreen shrubs/ 10°F/–12°C (most)	White, pink, red
CAMPANULA Bellflower	p. 71	Deciduous and evergreen perennials/ –30°F/–34°C (most)	White, pink, blue
CERCIS canadensis Eastern redbud	p. 74	Deciduous tree/ –20°F/–29°C	White, pink, red
CIMICIFUGA Bugbane	p. 74	Deciduous perennials/ –35°F/–37°C	White
CLEMATIS Clematis	p. 75	Deciduous and evergreen vines/ –20°F/–29°C (most)	White, yellow, pink, red, violet, purple, blue
CLETHRA alnifolia Summersweet, sweet pepperbush	p. 75	Deciduous shrub/ –40°F/–40°C	White, pink
CLIVIA miniata Clivia, Kaffir lily	p. 75	Evergreen perennial/ 25°F/–4°C	Yellow, orange, red
CONVALLARIA majalis Lily-of-the-valley	p. 76	Deciduous perennial/ –40°F/–40°C	White, pink
CORNUS Dogwood	p. 76	Deciduous trees, shrubs, perennial/ Varies	White, pink
CORYDALIS lutea Corydalis	p. 77	Deciduous perennial/ –10°F/–23°C	Yellow
COTULA squalida New Zealand brass buttons	p. 77	Evergreen to deciduous perennial ground cover/ –10°F/–23°C	Yellow
CYCLAMEN Cyclamen	p. 77	Deciduous tuberous perennials/ 0°F/–18°C	White, pink, red, lilac
CYMBALARIA muralis Kenilworth ivy	p. 79	Evergreen perennial/ –20°F/–29°C	White, lavender
DAPHNE Daphne	p. 79	Deciduous and evergreen shrubs/ Varies	White, pink
DICENTRA Bleeding heart	p. 80	Deciduous perennials/ –35°F/–37°C	White, pink

TROLLIUS chinensis

THALICTRUM aquilegifolium

		TYPE/ HARDINESS	FRUIT COLOR
DIGITALIS Foxglove	p. 80	Evergreen biennial and perennials/ Varies	White, yellow, pink, purple, lavender
DORONICUM Leopard's bane	p. 80	Deciduous perennials/ −30°F/−34°C	Yellow
DUCHESNEA indica Indian mock strawberry	p. 80	Evergreen perennial ground cover/ −30°F/−34°C	Yellow
ENKIANTHUS Enkianthus	p. 81	Deciduous shrubs/ Varies	White, yellow, red
EPIMEDIUM Epimedium, barrenwort, bishop's hat	p. 81	Deciduous and evergreen perennials/ −30°F/−34°C	White, yellow, pink, red, lavender
FILIPENDULA Meadowsweet	p.83	Deciduous perennials/ Varies	Pink, white
FOTHERGILLA Fothergilla	p. 83	Deciduous shrubs/ −10°F/−23°C	White
FRANCOA ramosa Bridal wreath, maiden's wreath	p. 83	Evergreen perennial/ 5°F/−15°C	White, pink
FRANKLINIA alatamaha Franklinia	p. 84	Deciduous tree/ −10°F/−23°C	White
FUCHSIA Fuchsia	p. 84	Deciduous to semi-evergreen shrubs/ Varies	White, orange, pink, red, purple
GALAX urceolata Wand flower	p. 84	Evergreen perennial/ −30°F/−34°C	White
GALIUM odoratum Sweet woodruff	p. 85	Evergreen perennial/ −20°F/−29°C	White
GAULTHERIA Gaultheria	p. 85	Evergreen shrubs, ground covers/ Varies	White, pink
GRASSES, ornamental (some)	p. 78	Evergreen and deciduous perennials/ Varies	White, pink
HALESIA Silver bell	p. 85	Deciduous trees/ −20°F/−29°C	White, pink
HAMAMELIS Witch hazel	p. 86	Deciduous shrubs/ Varies	Yellow, orange, red

		TYPE/ HARDINESS	FRUIT COLOR
HELLEBORUS Hellebore	p. 87	Deciduous and evergreen perennials/ Varies	White, cream, pink, maroon, green
HEMEROCALLIS Daylily	p. 87	Deciduous and evergreen perennials/ Varies	Many colors
× HEUCHERELLA tiarelloides Heucherella	p. 87	Evergreen perennial/ −20°F/−29°C	Pink
HOSTA Hosta, plantain lily, funkia	p. 88	Deciduous perennials/ −35°F/−37°C	White, lilac, violet
HYDRANGEA Hydrangea	p. 88	Deciduous shrubs and vine/ Varies	White, pink, red, blue
HYPERICUM St. Johnswort	p. 89	Evergreen shrubs and ground cover/ Varies	Yellow
IRIS foetidissima Gladwin iris	p. 90	Evergreen perennial/ 0°F/−18°C	Gray/tan, lavender, yellow
KALMIA latifolia Mountain laurel, calico bush	p. 90	Evergreen shrub/ −20°F/−29°C	White, pink, red
KERRIA japonica Kerria	p. 91	Deciduous shrub/ −20°F/−29°C	Yellow
LAMIUM Dead nettle	p. 91	Deciduous to evergreen perennials/ −20°F/−29°C	White, yellow, pink
LEUCOTHOE fontanesiana Drooping leucothoe	p. 92	Evergreen shrub/ −20°F/−29°C	White
LIGULARIA Ligularia	p. 92	Deciduous perennials/ −30°F/−34°C	Yellow
LILIUM Lily	p. 92	Deciduous (bulb)/ Varies	Many colors
LIRIOPE/OPHIOPOGON Lily turf	p. 93	Evergreen perennials/ −10°F/−23°C (most)	White, lilac, violet
LONICERA Honeysuckle	p. 93	Deciduous to evergreen vines/ Varies	White, cream, yellow, orange, pink, red, purple
LYSIMACHIA nummularia Creeping Jenny, moneywort	p. 94	Evergreen perennial/ −30°F/−34°C	Yellow

KALMIA *latifolia*

DIGITALIS *purpurea*

	TYPE/ HARDINESS	FLOWER COLOR
MAHONIA p. 94 Mahonia	Evergreen shrubs/ Varies	Yellow
MERTENSIA p. 95 Bluebells	Deciduous perennials/ −35°F/−37°C	Blue
MYOSOTIS scorpioides p. 95 Forget-me-not	Deciduous to evergreen perennial/ −20°F/−29°C	White, pink, blue
MYRTUS communis p. 95 Myrtle	Evergreen shrub/ 15°F/−9°C	White
NANDINA domestica p. 96 Heavenly bamboo, nandina	Evergreen shrub/ 0°F/−18°C	White
OSMANTHUS p. 96 Osmanthus	Evergreen shrubs/ 0°F/−18°C (most)	White, orange
PACHYSANDRA p. 96 terminalis Japanese spurge	Evergreen subshrub/ −20°F/−29°C	White
PIERIS p. 97 Pieris	Evergreen shrubs/ Varies	White, pink, red
PITTOSPORUM p. 98 Pittosporum	Evergreen trees and shrubs/ Varies	White, yellow, purple
PLATYCODON p. 98 grandiflorus Balloon flower	Deciduous perennial/ −35°F/−37°C	White, pink, blue
POLEMONIUM p. 99 caeruleum Jacob's ladder	Deciduous perennials/ −40°F/−40°C	White, blue
POLYGONATUM p. 99 Solomon's seal	Deciduous perennials/ −30°F/−34°C	White
PRIMULA p. 99 Primrose	Evergreen and deciduous perennials/ −20°F/−29°C (most)	Many colors
PRUNELLA p. 100 Self-heal	Evergreen perennials/ −20°F/−29°C	White, pink, purple, lilac
PULMONARIA p. 101 Lungwort	Deciduous and evergreen perennials/ −35°F/−37°C (most)	White, pink, blue

	TYPE/ HARDINESS	FLOWER COLOR
RHAPHIOLEPIS indica p. 102 Rhaphiolepis, India hawthorn	Evergreen shrub/ 10°F/−12°C	White, pink, red
RHODODENDRON p. 102 Rhododendron, azalea	Deciduous and evergreen shrubs/ Varies	Many colors
RIBES sanguineum p. 103 Pink winter currant, red flowering currant	Deciduous shrub/ 0F°/−18°C	White, pink, red
SKIMMIA p. 104 Skimmia	Evergreen shrubs/ 0°F/−18°C	White
STEWARTIA p. 105 Stewartia	Deciduous trees/ −10°F/−23°C	White
THALICTRUM p. 106 Meadow rue	Deciduous perennials/ −20°F/−29°C	Yellow, lilac, violet
TIARELLA p. 106 Tiarella, false miterwort	Deciduous to evergreen perennials/ Varies	White, pink
TRACHELOSPERMUM p. 107 jasminoides Star jasmine, Confederate jasmine	Evergreen vine/ 15°F/−9°C	White
TRADESCANTIA p. 107 × andersoniana Spiderwort	Deciduous perennial/ −20°F/−29°C	White, pink, purple, lilac, blue
TRICYRTIS p. 107 Toad lily	Deciduous perennials/ 0°F/−18°C	White, purple- spotted, lilac
TRILLIUM p. 108 Trillium, wake robin	Deciduous perennials/ Varies	White, yellow, pink, maroon
TROLLIUS p. 108 Globeflower	Deciduous perennials/ −30°F/−34°C	Yellow, orange
VANCOUVERIA p. 109 Vancouveria	Deciduous and evergreen perennials/ 0°F/−18°C	White, yellow
VIBURNUM p. 109 Viburnum	Deciduous and evergreen shrubs/ Varies	White, pink
VIOLA p. 110 Violet	Deciduous and evergreen perennials/ Varies	White, pink, purple, lilac, blue

Shade Plants with Colorful Fruits

Fruiting plants offer polka-dots of color to sparkle up shade gardens. And most of these fruits are colorful in autumn and winter, when flower color is at low ebb.

AUCUBA japonica 'Picturata'

SKIMMIA japonica

		TYPE/ HARDINESS	FRUIT COLOR
AKEBIA quinata Fiveleaf akebia	p. 62	Deciduous to semi-evergreen vine/ −30°F/−34°C	Purple
AMPELOPSIS brevipedunculata Blueberry climber	p. 63	Deciduous vine/ −30°F/−34°C	White to blue
ARBUTUS unedo Strawberry tree	p. 64	Evergreen tree, shrub/ 5°F/−15°C	Yellow, red
ARDISIA Ardisia	p. 64	Evergreen shrubs/ Varies	Red
AUCUBA japonica Japanese aucuba	p. 66	Evergreen shrub/ 0°F/−18°C	Pinkish buff, red
BERBERIS Barberry	p. 68	Deciduous and evergreen shrubs/ Varies	Red, violet, dark blue, black
CORNUS Dogwood	p. 76	Deciduous trees, shrubs, perennial/ Varies	Red
DAPHNE (some) Daphne	p. 79	Deciduous and evergreen shrubs/ Varies	White, yellow, red
DUCHESNEA indica Indian mock strawberry	p. 80	Evergreen perennial ground cover/ −30°F/−34°C	Red
EUONYMUS fortunei (some) Euonymus	p. 82	Evergreen shrub and vine/ −20°F/−29°C	Orange
GAULTHERIA Gaultheria	p. 85	Evergreen shrubs, ground covers/ Varies	Red, black
ILEX Holly	p. 89	Deciduous and evergreen shrubs/ Varies	White, yellow, orange, red, black
IRIS foetidissima Gladwin iris	p. 90	Evergreen perennial/ 0°F/−18°C	Orange-red
LIRIOPE/OPHIOPOGON Lily turf	p. 93	Evergreen perennials/ −10°F/−23°C (most)	Blue
LONICERA (most) Honeysuckle	p. 93	Evergreen to deciduous vines/ Varies	Red
MAHONIA Mahonia	p. 94	Evergreen shrubs/ Varies	Red, blue, blue-black
MYRTUS communis Myrtle	p. 95	Evergreen shrub/ 15°F/−9°C	Black

		TYPE/ HARDINESS	FRUIT COLOR
NANDINA domestica Heavenly bamboo, nandina	p. 96	Evergreen shrub/ 0°F/−18°C	Red
PACHYSANDRA terminalis Japanese spurge	p. 96	Evergreen subshrub/ −20°F/−29°C	White
PARTHENOCISSUS Woodbine	p. 97	Deciduous vines/ Varies	Blue-black
PITTOSPORUM tobira Tobira	p. 98	Evergreen shrub/ −5°F/−21°C	Orange
RHAMNUS Buckthorn	p. 101	Deciduous and evergreen shrubs/ Varies	Yellow, red to black, black
RIBES sanguineum Pink winter currant, red flowering currant	p. 103	Deciduous shrub/ 0°F/−18°C	Blue-black
RUBUS pentalobus Taiwan bramble	p. 103	Evergreen ground cover shrub/ 0°F/−18°C	Salmon
RUSCUS Butcher's broom	p.103	Evergreen shrubs/ 0°F/−18°C	Red
SARCOCOCCA Sweet box, sarcococca	p. 104	Evergreen shrubs/ 0°F/−18°C	Red, blue-black, black
SKIMMIA Skimmia	p. 104	Evergreen shrubs/ 0°F/−18°C	Red
TAXUS Yew	p. 105	Evergreen shrubs/ Varies	Red
VIBURNUM Viburnum	p. 109	Deciduous and evergreen shrubs/ Varies	Red, blue, black

Autumn Foliage Color in Shade

For some plants, autumn foliage is a second burst of color after spring or summer blossoms. Others present colorful foliage and fruits together. And a few individuals vary otherwise all-green existences by this one-time annual color extravaganza.

ACER palmatum and deciduous azaleas (Rhododendron)

PARTHENOCISSUS quinquefolia

		TYPE/ HARDINESS	FOLIAGE COLOR
ACER Maple	p. 58	Deciduous trees/ Varies	Yellow, orange, red
AMPELOPSIS brevipedunculata Blueberry climber	p. 63	Deciduous vine/ −30°F/−34°C	Red
BERBERIS (some) Barberry	p. 68	Deciduous shrubs/ Varies	Yellow, orange red
CERCIDIPHYLLUM japonicum Katsura tree	p. 74	Deciduous tree/ −30°F/−34°C	Yellow, red
CERCIS canadensis Eastern redbud	p. 74	Deciduous tree/ −20°F/−29°C	Yellow
CLETHRA alnifolia Summersweet, sweet pepperbush	p. 75	Deciduous shrub/ −40°F/−40°C	Yellow, orange
CORNUS Dogwood	p. 76	Deciduous trees, shrubs, perennial/ Varies	Yellow, orange, red
ENKIANTHUS Enkianthus	p. 81	Deciduous shrubs/ Varies	Orange, red
EPIMEDIUM Epimedium, barrenwort, bishop's hat	p. 81	Deciduous and evergreen perennials/ −30°F/−34°C	Reddish bronze
FOTHERGILLA Fothergilla	p. 83	Deciduous shrubs/ −10°F/−23°C	Yellow, orange, red-purple
FRANKLINIA alatamaha Franklinia	p. 84	Deciduous tree/ −10°F/−23°C	Red
GALAX urceolata Wand flower	p. 84	Evergreen perennial/ −30°F/−34°C	Bronze

		TYPE/ HARDINESS	FOLIAGE COLOR
HALESIA Silver bell	p. 85	Deciduous trees/ −20°F/−29°C	Yellow
HAMAMELIS Witch hazel	p. 86	Deciduous shrubs/ Varies	Yellow, orange, red
HYDRANGEA (some) Hydrangea	p. 88	Deciduous shrubs/ Varies	Bronzy red, bronze
ILEX verticillata Winterberry	p. 89	Deciduous shrub/ −30°F/−34°C	Yellow
KERRIA japonica Kerria	p. 91	Deciduous shrub/ −20°F/−29°C	Yellow
LEUCOTHOE fontanesiana Drooping leucothoe	p. 92	Evergreen shrub/ −20°F/−29°C	Bronze-purple
MAHONIA aquifolium Oregon grape	p. 94	Evergreen shrub/ −10°F/−23°C	Bronze-purple
NANDINA domestica Heavenly bamboo, nandina	p. 96	Evergreen shrub/ 0°F/−18°C	Red
PARTHENOCISSUS Woodbine	p. 97	Deciduous vines/ Varies	Red, burgundy
RHAMNUS frangula Alder buckthorn	p. 101	Deciduous shrub/ −40°F/−40°C	Yellow
RHODODENDRON Azalea (deciduous)	p. 102	Deciduous shrubs/ Varies	Yellow, orange, red, maroon
RIBES sanguineum Winter currant	p. 103	Deciduous shrub/ 0°F/−18°C	Rusty yellow
STEWARTIA Stewartia	p. 105	Deciduous trees/ −10°F/−23°C	Orange, red, purple, bronze
VIBURNUM (some) Viburnum	p. 109	Deciduous shrubs/ Varies	Red, red-purple

Container Plants for Shade

For the shaded patio, terrace, or deck, container plants may provide the entire landscape. And even in a shaded garden in the ground, one plant in a special container can be an arresting focal point. Here is a range of shade plants that will grow well with their roots confined. All the annuals listed on pages 60–61 also make good container plants.

Hosta and Japanese forest grass (Hakonechloa)

		TYPE/ HARDINESS	FLOWER COLOR
ABUTILON Flowering maple	p. 58	Evergreen shrubs/ 25°F/–4°C	White, yellow, orange, pink, red
ACER Maple	p. 59	Deciduous trees/ –10°F/–23°C	
ARBUTUS unedo (some) Strawberry tree	p. 64	Evergreen tree, shrub/ 5°F/–15°C	
ASPIDISTRA elatior Aspidistra, cast-iron plant	p. 65	Evergreen perennial/ 5°F/–15°C	
AUCUBA japonica Japanese aucuba	p. 66	Evergreen shrub/ 0°F/–18°C	
BEGONIA × tuberhybrida Tuberous begonia	p. 68	Deciduous tuberous perennial/ Tender	White, cream, yellow, orange, pink, red
BERGENIA Bergenia	p. 69	Deciduous and evergreen perennials/ Varies	White, pink, rosy purple, magenta
CALADIUM bicolor Caladium, fancy-leafed caladium	p. 70	Deciduous tuberous perennial/ Tender	
CAMELLIA Camellia	p. 71	Evergreen shrubs/ 10°F/–12°C (most)	White, pink, red,
CLIVIA miniata Clivia, Kaffir lily	p. 75	Evergreen perennial/ 25°F/–4°C	Yellow, orange, red
CYCLAMEN Cyclamen	p. 77	Deciduous tuberous perennials/ 0°F/–18°C	White, pink, red, lilac
× FATSHEDERA lizei Fatshedera	p. 82	Evergreen vining shrub/ 5°F/–15°C	
FATSIA japonica Japanese aralia	p. 82	Evergreen shrub/ 5°F/–15°C	
FERNS	p. 72	Deciduous and evergreen perennials/ Varies	

		TYPE/ HARDINESS	FLOWER COLOR
FUCHSIA Fuchsia	p. 84	Deciduous to semi-evergreen shrubs/ Varies	White, orange, pink, red, purple
HEDERA Ivy	p. 86	Evergreen vines/ Varies	
HOSTA Hosta, plantain lily, funkia	p. 88	Deciduous perennials/ –35°F/–37°C	White, lilac, violet
HYDRANGEA macrophylla Bigleaf hydrangea	p. 88	Deciduous shrub/ –10°F/–23°C	White, pink, red, blue
LAMIUM Dead nettle	p. 91	Deciduous to evergreen perennials/ –20°F/–29°C	White, yellow, pink
LAURUS nobilis Sweet bay, Grecian laurel	p. 91	Evergreen tree or shrub/ 10°F/–12°C	
LIRIOPE/OPHIOPOGON Lily turf	p. 93	Evergreen perennials/ –10°F/–23°C (most)	White, lilac, violet
MAHONIA bealei Leatherleaf mahonia	p. 94	Evergreen shrub/ 0°F/–18°C	Yellow
NANDINA domestica Heavenly bamboo, nandina	p. 96	Evergreen shrub/ 0°F/–18°C	White
PITTOSPORUM tobira Tobira	p. 98	Evergreen shrub/ –5°F/–21°C	White
PRIMULA Primrose	p. 99	Deciduous and evergreen perennials/ –20°F/–29°C (most)	Many colors
RHAPHIOLEPIS indica Rhaphiolepis, India hawthorn	p. 102	Evergreen shrub/ 10°F/–12°C	White, pink, red
RHODODENDRON Rhododendron, azalea	p. 102	Deciduous and evergreen shrubs/ Varies	Many colors
TAXUS Yew	p. 105	Evergreen shrubs/ Varies	

Shade-loving Perennials

ALCHEMILLA mollis

The world of perennials holds an endless diversity of plants. Many are noted for floral display, some simply for beauty of foliage. The shade garden offers a congenial home to both types. For perennials used as ground covers, see page 48.

		TYPE/ HARDINESS	FLOWER COLOR
ACANTHUS mollis Acanthus, bear's breech	p. 58	Evergreen/ 0°F/−18°C	Purple and white
ACONITUM Aconite, monkshood	p. 59	Deciduous/ −30°F/−34°C	White, pink, violet, blue
ALCHEMILLA mollis Lady's mantle	p. 62	Deciduous to semi-evergreen/ −40°F/−40°C	Yellow-green
ANEMONE × hybrida Japanese anemone	p. 63	Semideciduous/ −20°F/−29°C	White, pink
AQUILEGIA Columbine	p. 63	Deciduous/ −35°F/−37°C (species), −20°F/−29°C (hybrids)	White, yellow, pink, red, purple, blue
ARUNCUS dioicus Goatsbeard	p. 64	Deciduous/ −35°F/−37°C	Cream
ASPIDISTRA elatior Aspidistra, cast-iron plant	p. 65	Evergreen/ 5°F/−15°C	
ASTILBE Astilbe, false spiraea, meadow sweet	p. 65	Deciduous/ −25°F/−32°C	White, pink, red, magenta
ASTRANTIA Masterwort	p. 66	Deciduous/ −10°F/−23°C	White, pink
BEGONIA × tuberhybrida Tuberous begonia	p. 68	Deciduous tuberous/ Tender	White, cream, yellow, orange, pink, red
BERGENIA Bergenia	p. 69	Deciduous and evergreen/ Varies	White, pink, rosy purple, magenta
BLETILLA striata Chinese ground orchid	p. 69	Deciduous/ 10°F/−12°C	White, lavender
BRUNNERA macrophylla Brunnera, Siberian bugloss	p. 69	Deciduous/ −35°F/−37°C	Blue
CALADIUM bicolor Caladium, fancy-leafed caladium	p. 70	Deciduous tuberous/ Tender	

		TYPE/ HARDINESS	FLOWER COLOR
CAMPANULA Bellflower	p. 71	Deciduous and evergreen/ −30°F/−34°C (most)	White, pink, blue
CLIVIA miniata Clivia, Kaffir lily	p. 75	Evergreen/ 25°F/−4°C	Yellow, orange, red
CONVALLARIA majalis Lily-of-the-valley	p. 76	Deciduous/ −40°F/−40°C	White, pink
CORYDALIS lutea Corydalis	p. 77	Deciduous/ −10°F/−23°C	Yellow
CYCLAMEN Cyclamen	p. 77	Deciduous tuberous/ 0°F/−18°C	White, pink, red, lilac
CYMBALARIA muralis Kenilworth ivy	p. 79	Evergreen/ −20°F/−29°C	White, lavender
DICENTRA Bleeding heart	p. 80	Deciduous/ −35°F/−37°C	White, pink
DIGITALIS Foxglove	p. 80	Evergreen/ Varies	White, yellow, pink, purple, lavender
DORONICUM Leopard's bane	p. 80	Deciduous/ −30°F/−34°C	Yellow
EPIMEDIUM Epimedium, barrenwort, bishop's hat	p. 81	Deciduous and evergreen/ −30°F/−34°C	White, yellow, pink, red, lavender
FERNS	p. 72	Deciduous and evergreen/ Varies	
FILIPENDULA Meadowsweet	p. 83	Deciduous/ Varies	White, pink
FRANCOA ramosa Bridal wreath, maiden's wreath	p. 83	Evergreen/ 5°F/−15°C	White, pink
GALAX urceolata Wand flower	p. 84	Evergreen/ −30°F/−34°C	White
GALIUM odoratum Sweet woodruff	p. 85	Evergreen/ −20°F/−29°C	White

THALICTRUM aquilegifolium　　　*TRILLIUM grandiflorum*　　　*ASTILBE × arendsii 'Glow'*

		TYPE/ HARDINESS	FLOWER COLOR
GRASSES, ornamental	p. 78	Deciduous and evergreen/ Varies	White, pink
HELLEBORUS Hellebore	p. 87	Deciduous and evergreen/ Varies	White, cream, pink, maroon, green
HEMEROCALLIS Daylily	p. 87	Deciduous and evergreen/ Varies	Many colors
× HEUCHERELLA tiarelloides Heucherella	p. 87	Evergreen/ −20°F/−29°C	Pink
HOSTA Hosta, plantain lily, funkia	p. 88	Deciduous/ −35°F/−37°C	White, lilac, violet
IRIS foetidissima Gladwin iris	p. 90	Evergreen/ 0°F/−18°C	Gray/tan, lavender, yellow
LAMIUM Dead nettle	p. 91	Deciduous to evergreen/ −20°F/−29°C	White, yellow, pink
LIGULARIA Ligularia	p. 92	Deciduous/ −30°F/−34°C	Yellow
LILIUM Lily	p. 92	Deciduous (bulb)/ Varies	Many colors
LIRIOPE/OPHIOPOGON Lily turf	p. 93	Evergreen/ −10°F/−23°C (most)	White, lilac, violet
MERTENSIA Bluebells	p. 95	Deciduous/ −35°F/−37°C	Blue
MYOSOTIS scorpioides Forget-me-not	p. 95	Deciduous to evergreen/ −20°F/−29°C	White, pink, blue
PLATYCODON grandiflorus Balloon flower	p. 98	Deciduous/ −35°F/−37°C	White, pink, blue

		TYPE/ HARDINESS	FLOWER COLOR
POLEMONIUM caeruleum Jacob's ladder	p. 99	Deciduous/ −40°F/−40°C	White, blue
POLYGONATUM Solomon's seal	p. 99	Deciduous/ −30°F/−34°C	White
PRIMULA Primrose	p. 99	Deciduous and evergreen/ −20°F/−29°C (most)	Many colors
PRUNELLA Self-heal	p. 100	Evergreen/ −20°F/−29°C	White, pink, purple, lilac
PULMONARIA Lungwort	p. 101	Deciduous and evergreen/ −35°F/−37°C (most)	White, pink, blue
THALICTRUM Meadow rue	p. 106	Deciduous/ −20°F/−29°C	Yellow, lilac, violet
TIARELLA Tiarella, false miterwort	p. 106	Deciduous to evergreen/ Varies	White, pink
TRADESCANTIA × andersoniana Spiderwort	p. 107	Deciduous/ −20°F/−29°C	White, pink, purple, lilac, blue
TRICYRTIS Toad lily	p. 107	Deciduous/ 0°F/−18°C	White, purple-spotted, lilac
TRILLIUM Trillium, wake robin	p. 108	Deciduous/ Varies	White, yellow, pink, maroon
TROLLIUS Globeflower	p. 108	Deciduous/ −30°F/−34°C	Yellow, orange
VANCOUVERIA Vancouveria	p. 109	Deciduous and evergreen/ 0°F/−18°C	White, yellow
VIOLA Violet	p. 110	Deciduous and evergreen/ Varies	White, pink, purple, lilac, blue

Ground Covers & Vines for Shade

Plants that blanket the ground or climb vertical surfaces can be the unifying element in any diverse planting. Ground covers may be the only plants that will grow beneath shallow-rooted trees. There is a great array of styles and textures for shade-scaping—from bold bergenia to diminutive baby's tears. Many vines can grow far and wide, casting shade of their own (see page 36). The vines here, though, will decorate shaded structures: trellises, walls, even tree trunks.

CORNUS canadensis

GROUND COVERS		TYPE/ HARDINESS	FLOWER COLOR
AEGOPODIUM podagraria Bishop's weed, gout weed	p. 62	Deciduous perennial/ –30°F/–34°C	
AJUGA reptans Ajuga, carpet bugle	p. 62	Evergreen perennial/ –30°F/–34°C	Blue
ARDISIA Ardisia	p. 64	Evergreen shrubs/ Varies	
ASARUM Wild ginger	p. 65	Deciduous and evergreen perennials/ Varies	
BERGENIA Bergenia	p. 69	Deciduous and evergreen perennials/ Varies	White, pink, rosy purple, magenta
CAMPANULA (some) Bellflower	p. 71	Deciduous and evergreen perennials/ –30°F/–34°C (most)	White, blue
CONVALLARIA majalis Lily-of-the-valley	p. 76	Deciduous perennial/ –40°F/–40°C	White, pink
CORNUS canadensis Bunchberry	p. 76	Deciduous perennial/ –40°F/–40°C	White
COTULA squalida New Zealand brass buttons	p. 77	Deciduous to evergreen perennial/ –10°F/–23°C	Yellow
CYMBALARIA muralis Kenilworth ivy	p. 79	Evergreen perennial/ –20°F/–29°C	White, lavender
DICENTRA (some) Bleeding heart	p. 80	Deciduous perennials/ –35°F/–37°C	White, pink
DUCHESNEA indica Indian mock strawberry	p. 81	Evergreen perennial/ –30°F/–34°C	Yellow
EPIMEDIUM Epimedium, barrenwort, bishop's hat	p. 81	Deciduous and evergreen perennials/ –30°F/–34°C	White, yellow, pink, red, lavender

GROUND COVERS		TYPE/ HARDINESS	FLOWER COLOR
× FATSHEDERA lizei Fatshedera	p. 82	Evergreen vine/ 5°F/–15°C	
GALAX urceolata Wand flower	p. 84	Evergreen perennial/ –30°F/–34°C	White
GALIUM odoratum Sweet woodruff	p. 85	Evergreen perennial/ –20°F/–29°C	White
GAULTHERIA (some) Gaultheria	p. 85	Evergreen shrubs/ Varies	White, pink
HAKONECHLOA macra 'Aureola' Japanese forest grass	p. 78	Evergreen perennial/ –30°F/–34°C	
HEDERA Ivy	p. 86	Evergreen vines/ Varies	
HYPERICUM calycinum Creeping St. Johnswort, Aaron's beard	p. 89	Evergreen perennial/ 0°F/–18°C	Yellow
JUNIPERUS (some) Juniper	p. 90	Evergreen shrubs/ Varies	
LAMIUM Dead nettle	p. 91	Deciduous to evergreen perennials/ –20°F/–29°C	White, yellow, pink
LIRIOPE/OPHIOPOGON Lily turf	p. 93	Evergreen perennials/ –10°F/–23°C (most)	White, lilac, violet
LYSIMACHIA nummularia Creeping Jenny, moneywort	p. 94	Evergreen perennial/ –30°F/–34°C	Yellow
MAHONIA (some) Mahonia	p. 94	Evergreen shrubs/ Varies	Yellow
MYOSOTIS scorpioides Forget-me-not	p. 95	Deciduous to evergreen perennial/ –20°F/–29°C	White, pink, blue

AJUGA reptans 'Burgundy Glow'

CLEMATIS montana

LONICERA × heckrottii

GROUND COVERS		TYPE/ HARDINESS	FLOWER COLOR
NANDINA domestica (some) Heavenly bamboo, nandina	p. 96	Evergreen shrub/ 0°F/−18°C	White
PACHYSANDRA terminalis Japanese spurge	p. 96	Evergreen subshrub/ −20°F/−29°C	
PRUNELLA Self-heal	p. 100	Evergreen perennials/ −20°F/−29°C	White, pink, purple, lilac
PULMONARIA Lungwort	p. 101	Deciduous and evergreen perennials/ Varies	White, pink, blue
RUBUS pentalobus Taiwan bramble	p. 103	Evergreen shrub/ 0°F/−18°C	White
SARCOCOCCA Sweet box, sarcococca	p. 104	Evergreen shrubs/ 0°F/−18°C	White
SKIMMIA Skimmia	p. 104	Evergreen shrubs/ 0°F/−18°C	White
SOLEIROLIA soleirolii Baby's tears, angel's tears	p. 105	Evergreen perennial/ 10°F/−12°C	
TIARELLA cordifolia Foamflower	p. 106	Deciduous to evergreen perennial/ −40°F/−40°C	White
TRACHELOSPERMUM jasminoides Star jasmine, Confederate jasmine	p. 107	Evergreen vine/ 15°F/−9°C	White
VANCOUVERIA Vancouveria	p. 109	Deciduous and evergreen perennials/ 0°F/−18°C	White, yellow
VIBURNUM davidii Viburnum	p. 109	Evergreen shrub/ 0°F/−18°C	White
VIOLA Violet	p. 110	Deciduous and evergreen perennials/ −10°F/−23°C (most)	White, pink, purple, lilac, blue

VINES		TYPE/ HARDINESS	FLOWER COLOR
ABUTILON megapotamicum Flowering maple	p. 58	Evergreen/ 25°F/−4°C	Yellow, yellow and red
ACTINIDIA kolomikta Actinidia	p. 59	Deciduous/ −30°F/−34°C	White
AKEBIA quinata Fiveleaf akebia	p. 62	Deciduous to semi-evergreen/ −30°F/−34°C	Purple
AMPELOPSIS brevipedunculata Blueberry climber	p. 63	Deciduous/ −30°F/−34°C	
CLEMATIS Clematis	p. 75	Deciduous and evergreen/ −20°F/−29°C (most)	White, yellow, pink, red, purple, violet
EUONYMUS fortunei (some) Euonymus	p. 82	Evergreen/ −20°F/−29°C	
× FATSHEDERA lizei Fatshedera	p. 82	Evergreen/ 5°F/−15°C	
HEDERA Ivy	p. 86	Evergreen/ Varies	
HYDRANGEA anomala petiolaris Climbing hydrangea	p. 88	Deciduous/ −20°F/−29°C	White
LONICERA Honeysuckle	p. 93	Deciduous to evergreen/ Varies	White, cream, yellow, orange, pink, red, purple
PARTHENOCISSUS Woodbine	p. 97	Deciduous/ Varies	
TRACHELOSPERMUM jasminoides Star jasmine, Confederate jasmine	p. 107	Evergreen/ 15°F/−9°C	White

Shade-tolerant Shrubs

In garden design, shrubs provide the backbone—the permanent plantings that influence views and direct your path through the garden.

FOTHERGILLA gardenii

PIERIS japonica

		TYPE/ HARDINESS	FLOWER COLOR
ABUTILON Flowering maple	p. 58	Evergreen/ 25°F/−4°C (most)	White, yellow, orange, pink, red
ACER palmatum (some) Japanese maple	p. 58	Deciduous/ −10°F/−23°C	
ARBUTUS unedo (some) Strawberry tree	p. 64	Evergreen/ 5°F/−15°C	White, pink
AUCUBA japonica Japanese aucuba	p. 66	Evergreen/ 0°F/−18°C	
AZARA Azara	p. 66	Evergreen/ Varies	Yellow
BERBERIS Barberry	p. 68	Deciduous and evergreen/ Varies	Yellow
BUXUS Boxwood	p. 70	Evergreen/ Varies	
CAMELLIA Camellia	p. 71	Evergreen/ 10°F/−12°C (most)	White, pink, red
CLETHRA alnifolia Summersweet, sweet pepperbush	p. 75	Deciduous/ −40°F/−40°C	White, pink
CORNUS (some) Dogwood	p. 76	Deciduous/ Varies	White
DAPHNE Daphne	p. 79	Deciduous and evergreen/ Varies	White, pink

		TYPE/ HARDINESS	FLOWER COLOR
ENKIANTHUS Enkianthus	p. 81	Deciduous/ Varies	White, yellow, red
EUONYMUS fortunei Euonymus	p. 82	Evergreen/ −20°F/−29°C	
FATSIA japonica Japanese aralia	p. 82	Evergreen/ 5°F/−15°C	White
FOTHERGILLA Fothergilla	p. 83	Deciduous/ −10°F/−23°C	White
FUCHSIA Fuchsia	p. 84	Deciduous to semi-evergreen/ Varies	White, pink, orange, red, purple
GAULTHERIA Gaultheria	p. 85	Evergreen/ Varies	White, pink
HAMAMELIS Witch hazel	p. 86	Deciduous/ Varies	Yellow, orange, red
HYDRANGEA Hydrangea	p. 88	Deciduous/ Varies	White, pink, red, blue
HYPERICUM St. Johnswort	p. 89	Evergreen/ Varies	Yellow
ILEX Holly	p. 89	Deciduous and evergreen/ Varies	
JUNIPERUS Juniper	p. 90	Evergreen/ Varies	

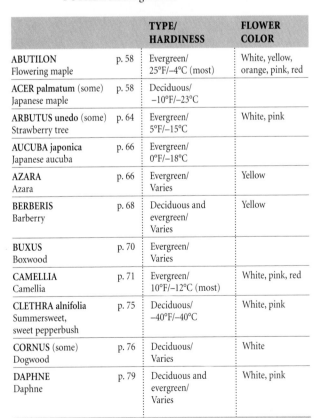

HYDRANGEA *quercifolia*

HYDRANGEA *macrophylla*

HAMAMELIS × *intermedia*
'Arnold Promise'

		TYPE/ HARDINESS	FLOWER COLOR
KALMIA latifolia Mountain laurel, calico bush	p. 90	Evergreen/ −20°F/−29°C	White, pink, red
KERRIA japonica Kerria	p. 91	Deciduous/ −20°F/−29°C	Yellow
LAURUS nobilis Sweet bay, Grecian laurel	p. 91	Evergreen/ 10°F/−12°C	
LEUCOTHOE fontanesiana Drooping leucothoe	p. 92	Evergreen/ −20°F/−29°C	White
MAHONIA Mahonia	p. 94	Evergreen/ Varies	Yellow
MYRTUS communis Myrtle	p. 95	Evergreen/ 15°F/−9°C	White
NANDINA domestica Heavenly bamboo, nandina	p. 96	Evergreen/ 0°F/−18°C	White
OSMANTHUS Osmanthus	p. 96	Evergreen/ 0°F/−18°C (most)	White
PIERIS Pieris	p. 97	Evergreen/ Varies	White, pink, red
PITTOSPORUM Pittosporum	p. 98	Evergreen/ Varies	White, yellow, purple
PODOCARPUS (some) Podocarpus	p. 98	Evergreen/ Varies	

		TYPE/ HARDINESS	FLOWER COLOR
RHAMNUS Buckthorn	p. 101	Deciduous and evergreen/ Varies	
RHAPHIOLEPIS indica Rhaphiolepis, India hawthorn	p. 102	Evergreen/ 10°F/−12°C	White, pink, red
RHODODENDRON Rhododendron, azalea	p. 102	Deciduous and evergreen/ Varies	Many colors
RIBES sanguineum Pink winter currant, red flowering currant	p. 103	Deciduous/ 0°F/−18°C	White, pink, red
RUSCUS Butcher's broom	p. 103	Evergreen/ 0°F/−18°C	
SARCOCOCCA Sweet box, sarcococca	p. 104	Evergreen/ 0°F/−18°C	
SKIMMIA Skimmia	p. 104	Evergreen/ 0°F/−18°C	White
TAXUS Yew	p. 105	Evergreen/ Varies	
TSUGA (some) Hemlock	p. 109	Evergreen/ Varies	
VIBURNUM Viburnum	p. 109	Deciduous and evergreen/ Varies	White, pink

Small Trees for Shade

*To add the dimension of height in the
shade, these small trees will do the job.
Use them at the forefront of a
taller woodland, within a
shaded patio, and in the open shade
of an urban garden.*

STEWARTIA koreana

ACER palmatum

		TYPE/ HARDINESS	FLOWER COLOR
ACER Maple	p. 58	Deciduous/ –10°F/–23°C (most)	
ARBUTUS unedo Strawberry tree	p. 64	Evergreen/ 5°F/–15°C	White, pink
CERCIDIPHYLLUM japonicum Katsura tree	p. 74	Deciduous/ –30°F/–34°C	Reddish purple
CERCIS canadensis Eastern redbud	p. 74	Deciduous/ –20°F/–29°C	White, pink, red, purplish pink
CORNUS (some) Dogwood	p. 76	Deciduous/ Varies	White, pink
FRANKLINIA alatamaha Franklinia	p. 84	Deciduous/ –10°F/–23°C	White
HALESIA Silver bell	p. 85	Deciduous/ –20°F/–29°C	White, pink

		TYPE/ HARDINESS	FLOWER COLOR
HYDRANGEA paniculata 'Grandiflora' Peegee hydrangea	p. 88	Deciduous/ –30°F/–34°C	White
ILEX (some) Holly	p. 89	Deciduous and evergreen/ Varies	
LAURUS nobilis Sweet bay, Grecian laurel	p. 91	Evergreen/ 10°F/–12°C	
PODOCARPUS (some) Podocarpus	p. 98	Evergreen/ Varies	
STEWARTIA Stewartia	p. 105	Deciduous/ –10°F/–23°C	White
TAXUS (some) Yew	p. 105	Evergreen/ Varies	
VIBURNUM lentago Nannyberry	p. 110	Deciduous/ –50°F/–46°C	White

Plants for Deep Shade

Lack of light is a daunting challenge for the majority of plants. Here are the stalwarts that will thrive in the equivalent of forest gloom.

ASARUM europaeum

Hosta collection

		TYPE/ HARDINESS	FLOWER COLOR
ARDISIA Ardisia	p. 64	Evergreen shrubs/ Varies	
ASARUM Wild ginger	p. 65	Deciduous and evergreen perennials/ Varies	
ASPIDISTRA elatior Aspidistra, cast-iron plant	p. 65	Evergreen perennial/ 5°F/–15°C	
AUCUBA japonica Japanese aucuba	p. 66	Evergreen shrub/ 0°F/–18°C	
BERGENIA Bergenia	p. 69	Deciduous and evergreen perennials/ Varies	White, pink, rosy purple, lilac
CLIVIA miniata Clivia, Kaffir lily	p. 75	Evergreen perennial/- 25°F/–4°C	Yellow, orange, red
✕ **FATSHEDERA lizei** Fatshedera	p. 82	Evergreen vining shrub/ 5°F/–15°C	
FATSIA japonica Japanese aralia	p. 82	Evergreen shrub/ 5°F/–15°C	
FERNS	p. 72	Deciduous and evergreen perennials/ Varies	
GALIUM odoratum Sweet woodruff	p. 85	Evergreen perennial/ –20°F/–29°C	White

		TYPE/ HARDINESS	FLOWER COLOR
HEDERA Ivy	p. 86	Evergreen vines/ Varies	
HOSTA Hosta, plantain lily, funkia	p. 88	Deciduous perennials/ –35°F/–37°C	White, lilac, violet
IRIS foetidissima Gladwin iris	p. 90	Evergreen perennial/ 0°F/–18°C	Gray/tan, lavender, yellow
NANDINA domestica Heavenly bamboo, nandina	p. 96	Evergreen shrub/ 0°F/–18°C	White
PACHYSANDRA terminalis Japanese spurge	p. 96	Evergreen subshrub/ –20°F/–29°C	White
POLYGONATUM Solomon's seal	p. 99	Deciduous perennials/ –30°F/–34°C	White
RUSCUS Butcher's broom	p. 103	Evergreen shrubs/ 0°F/–18°C	
SARCOCOCCA Sweet box, sarcococca	p. 104	Evergreen shrubs/ 0°F/–18°C	White
SOLEIROLIA soleirolii Baby's tears, angel's tears	p. 105	Evergreen perennial/ 10°F/–12°C	
TAXUS Yew	p. 105	Evergreen shrubs (most)/ Varies	

Shade Plants for Moist Soil

Unlike the many plants that need
"well-drained soil," these actually prefer
a soil that is constantly moist.
They'll thrive at the margin of a pond
—or in a well-watered bed.

LIGULARIA dentata

ARUNCUS dioicus

CLETHRA alnifolia

		TYPE/ HARDINESS	FLOWER COLOR
ARDISIA Ardisia	p. 64	Evergreen shrubs/ Varies	
ARUNCUS dioicus Goatsbeard	p. 64	Deciduous perennial/ −35°F/−37°C	Cream
ASARUM Wild ginger	p. 65	Deciduous and evergreen perennials/ Varies	
ASTILBE Astilbe, false spiraea, meadow sweet	p. 65	Deciduous perennials/ −25°F/−32°C	White, pink, red, magenta
CAREX Sedge	p. 78	Evergreen perennials/ −20°F/−29°C	
CLETHRA alnifolia Summersweet, sweet pepperbush	p. 75	Deciduous shrub/ −40°F/−40°C	White, pink
CORNUS (some) Dogwood	p. 76	Deciduous shrubs/ Varies	White, pink

		TYPE/ HARDINESS	FLOWER COLOR
FILIPENDULA Meadowsweet	p. 83	Deciduous perennials/ Varies	White, pink
HOSTA Hosta, plantain lily, funkia	p. 88	Deciduous perennials/ −35°F/−37°C	White, lilac, violet
LIGULARIA Ligularia	p. 92	Deciduous perennials/ −30°F/−34°C (most)	Yellow
LYSIMACHIA nummularia Creeping Jenny, moneywort	p. 94	Evergreen perennial/ −30°F/−34°C	Yellow
PRIMULA (some) Primrose	p. 99	Deciduous and evergreen perennials/ −20°F/−29°C (most)	Many colors
TRADESCANTIA × andersoniana Spiderwort	p. 107	Deciduous perennial/ −20°F/−29°C	White, pink, purple, lilac, blue
TROLLIUS Globeflower	p. 108	Deciduous perennials/ −30°F/−34°C	Yellow, orange

Shade Plants for Dry Soil

ARBUTUS unedo

"Dry shade" is a vexing problem with a limited number of plants as solutions. Here is a roster of proven successes for those shaded places beyond the reach of a hose.

OSMANTHUS heterophyllus

		TYPE/ HARDINESS	FLOWER COLOR
ARBUTUS unedo Strawberry tree	p. 64	Evergreen tree, shrub/ 5°F/–15°C	White, pink
ASPIDISTRA elatior Aspidistra, cast-iron plant	p. 65	Evergreen perennial/ 5°F/–15°C	
AUCUBA japonica Japanese aucuba	p. 66	Evergreen shrub/ 0°F/–18°C	
BERBERIS Barberry	p. 68	Deciduous and evergreen shrubs/ Varies	Yellow
BERGENIA Bergenia	p. 69	Deciduous and evergreen perennials/ Varies	White, pink, rosy purple, lilac
EUONYMUS fortunei Euonymus	p. 82	Evergreen shrub and vine/ –20°F/–29°C	
HEDERA Ivy	p. 86	Evergreen vines/ Varies	
HYPERICUM calycinum Creeping St. Johnswort, Aaron's beard	p. 89	Evergreen ground cover/ 0°F/–18°C	Yellow
IRIS foetidissima Gladwin iris	p. 90	Evergreen perennial/ 0°F/–18°C	Gray/tan, lavender, yellow
JUNIPERUS Juniper	p. 90	Evergreen shrub/ Varies	
LAURUS nobilis Sweet bay, Grecian laurel	p. 91	Evergreen tree or shrub/ 10°F/–12°C	

		TYPE/ HARDINESS	FLOWER COLOR
MAHONIA (most) Mahonia	p. 94	Evergreen shrubs/ Varies	Yellow
MYRTUS communis Myrtle	p. 95	Evergreen shrub/ 15°F/–9°C	White
NANDINA domestica Heavenly bamboo, nandina	p. 96	Evergreen shrub/ 0°F/–18°C	White
OSMANTHUS Osmanthus	p. 96	Evergreen shrub/ 0°F/–18°C (most)	White, orange
RHAMNUS Buckthorn	p. 101	Deciduous and evergreen shrubs/ Varies	
RIBES sanguineum Pink winter currant, red flowering currant	p. 103	Deciduous shrub/ 0°F/–18°C	White, pink, red
RUBUS pentalobus Taiwan bramble	p. 103	Evergreen ground cover shrub/ 0°F/–18°C	White
RUSCUS Butcher's broom	p. 103	Evergreen shrubs/ 0°F/–18°C	
TAXUS Yew	p. 105	Evergreen shrubs/ Varies	
VANCOUVERIA Vancouveria	p. 109	Deciduous and evergreen perennials/ 0°F/–18°C	White, yellow

ENCYCLOPEDIA OF SHADE PLANTS

The shade plants you select for your garden will give it that special character and form that make it pleasant to look at as well as comfortable to be in. From hosta glen to daphne bower to rhododendron dell, shade plants display their beauties in delightfully varied ways. • In the encyclopedia descriptions that follow, you'll find plants of all kinds. Tall or short, dense or open, with or without flowers—each can be the perfect choice for a shade garden somewhere. With these plant profiles and the guidelines presented in the previous chapters, you'll be able to compile a selection of plants just right for your landscape.

Massed flower clusters of Hydrangea macrophylla hybrids form a tapestry of harmonious colors in the shade.

ABUTILON

Flowering maple
Evergreen shrubs
Hardy to 25°F/–4°C except as noted
Part shade/regular water

From the flowers, you would correctly guess that this plant is related to hollyhock and hibiscus. The lobed leaves make it resemble maples—without any kinship despite the common name.

ABUTILON × hybridum

Widely grown *A. × hybridum* often goes by the name "Chinese lantern," which gives a picture of the bell-shaped blossoms that open from puffy, pendent buds. Petals of white, yellow, pink, orange, or red are attractively veined. Spring is the main flowering season, but a scattering of blooms occurs throughout summer; white- and yellow-flowered plants tend to bloom the longest. Rangy growth is upright or arching, to 10 feet high and wide. For creamy yellow–variegated leaves, look for *A. pictum* 'Thompsonii'; its pale orange flowers are veined in red.

Abutilon megapotamicum is a lax, almost vinelike plant good for espalier, growing through other shrubs, or hanging basket display. Funnel-like "lantern" flowers have yellow petals emerging from a red calyx; 'Marianne' has larger flowers, 'Variegata' features yellow-mottled leaves, and compact 'Victory' has small, darker yellow blossoms.

Gray-green leaves like grape foliage identify *A. vitifolium*, hardy to about 10°F/–12°C. Plants are bushier than *A. × hybridum*, can grow 15 feet high, and bear saucerlike blue or white flowers to 3 inches across. Best growth is in the cool humidity of the West Coast and Pacific Northwest.

Culture. All flowering maples do best with good soil and regular watering. Pinch back new growth to encourage bushiness. Grow in containers in regions beyond their hardiness limitations.

Good companions. *Asarum, Aspidistra, Clivia, Hemerocallis, Podocarpus.*

ACANTHUS mollis

Acanthus, bear's breech
Evergreen perennial
Hardy to 0°F/–18°C
Part shade/moderate to regular water

Without its flowers, an acanthus clump could pass for a fancy rhubarb. Long-stalked, glossy 2-foot leaves are deeply dissected into many lobes. But then in late spring and early summer, foxglove-like flowering spikes rise 3 to 4 feet above the foliage mounds. The purple-hooded white flowers resemble snapdragons, nestled above greenish, spiny-toothed bracts.

Culture. Maximum light encourages the best flowering, but in all but cool-summer regions you need to plant acanthus in partial or light shade to keep leaves from wilting. Plants grow robustly in good, well-drained soil with regular watering, but they will endure poor soil and dryness at the expense of appearance.

Clumps will thrive undisturbed for many years. If you need to dig or divide plants, do it in midautumn through winter in mild-winter regions, early spring in colder areas. New plants will sprout from any portion of cut root, so avoid cultivating around clumps, and try to remove all roots from the soil when you dig plants.

ACANTHUS mollis

Good companions. *Ampelopsis, Euonymus, Laurus, Myrtus, Pittosporum, Taxus.*

ACER

Maple
Deciduous trees and shrubs
Hardy to –10°F/–23°C except as noted
Part shade/moderate to regular water

Most maples are medium-size to large trees that produce shade. But several of the most elegant species will thrive in the dappled or light shade of larger trees—or the afternoon shadow cast by structures.

Japanese maple *(A. palmatum)* comes in an almost bewildering array of foliage types, colors, and growth habits. But the basic species is a thing of beauty in itself. Trees may be rounded, spreading, even vase-shaped to 30 feet tall, often with multiple trunks or branching close to the ground. Foliage is carried in horizontal layers, each leaf 2 to 4 inches across with 5 or 7 lobes. Autumn color blazes yellow, orange, or red. Named selections may have dissected and variantly lobed leaves; smaller or larger leaves; dark red, bronze, or variegated foliage; colored bark; and such divergent forms as mop-headed shrubs.

ACER palmatum 'Sango Kaku'

Fullmoon maple (*A. japonicum*) looks like a Japanese maple with slightly larger leaves. Trees can reach the same size (though more slowly), bearing nearly circular leaves with up to 11 shallow lobes. The selection 'Aconitifolium' has deeply lobed and dissected leaves. Foliage of golden fullmoon maple (*A. shirasawanum* 'Aureum') emerges yellow and ages to chartreuse by summer. Both variants are slow-growing, best treated as modest-sized accent shrubs.

Vine maple (*A. circinatum*) is famous in its native Pacific Northwest for autumn foliage pyrotechnics at forest margins. More cold-tolerant than Japanese and fullmoon maples, it can take temperatures to –20°F/–29°C. In shade, growth is irregular, crooked, full of character. In the open, vine maples are upright and fairly symmetrical, similar to Japanese maples in size. Leaves are nearly circular, to 6 inches across with as many as 11 lobes. Yellow is the prevailing autumn color in shade; red is common if trees get more sun and winter chill. The selection 'Monroe' is a shrubby variant with deeply dissected foliage.

Culture. Best conditions for maples are good, well-drained soil and regular watering during dry periods to support the abundant foliage. The fairly thin leaves luxuriate in humidity—either warm or cool. Still, Japanese and vine maples are surprisingly adaptable, able to endure dry soil (if it is cool) and dry air (especially if lightly shaded). Root

ACONITUM 'Bressingham Spire'

systems tend to be shallow and fibrous, offering some competition to nearby plants.

Good companions. *Berberis, Euonymus, Helleborus, Hosta, Hydrangea, Juniperus, Mahonia.*

🌺
ACONITUM

Aconite, monkshood
Deciduous perennials
Hardy to –30°F/–34°C
Part shade/regular water

Consider the monkshoods a delphinium substitute for the lightly shaded garden. They give you a similar foliage effect—clumps of dark green, celerylike leaves that grow from tuberous roots—and blossoms of vivid blue, purple, or white rising in narrow spires. Each flower features a helmet- or hood-shaped, petal-like sepal, which accounts for the common name. Flowering time is summer to early autumn. *Note:* all plant parts are poisonous to ingest.

Specialty and perennials nurseries offer various species and hybrids. Plants sold as *A. bicolor* (now *A.* × *cammarum*) include 3-foot 'Bressingham Blue', with deep violet flowers, and 4-foot 'Bicolor', which has blossoms of blue and white. *Aconitum napellus* grows 3 to 5 feet tall, typically bearing blue or violet flowers, though specialists carry named selections in white and pink. Extending the bloom season into early autumn, *A. carmichaelii* (*A. fischeri*) and its selections offer blue to violet blossoms on 2- to 4-foot stems—up to 6 feet in *A. c.* 'Wilsonii'.

Culture. Monkshoods need many of the conditions that suit delphiniums: fertile, well-drained soil; regular moisture; and fairly cool, moist summers. Summer heat or dryness significantly degrades performance. And all monkshoods need some subfreezing winter temperatures in order to grow vigorously from year to year.

Good companions. *Astilbe, ferns, Galax, Hosta, Pulmonaria, Thalictrum.*

🌺
ACTINIDIA kolomikta

Actinidia
Deciduous vine
Hardy to –30°F/–34°C
Part shade/regular water

What this relative of kiwi fruit lacks in edible potential it makes up for in looks. A mass of 5-inch heart-shaped leaves presents a unique color display. Some leaves will be all green, others green

ACTINIDIA kolomikta

splashed with white, and still others strikingly variegated in pink to nearly red. The twining stems grow to 15 feet, also bearing fragrant white blossoms in summer.

Male and female flowers grow on separate plants, the male plants giving the better foliage. When both sexes are planted near one another, you may get inch-long yellow fruits.

Culture. Plant in good, well-drained soil, and water regularly during dry periods. Train and tie vines during the growing season; prune to shape during the leafless period before spring growth begins.

Good companions. *Anemone, Hydrangea, Kalmia, Rhododendron (particularly azaleas), Thalictrum.*

BEGONIA semperflorens-cultorum

BEGONIA semperflorens-cultorum • Bedding begonia, fibrous begonia

What it may lack in flashy color, bedding begonia more than makes up for in dependable performance. Bushy, dense plants have fleshy, crisp green or bronze leaves; overall height is 6 to 12 inches. Clustered flowers may be white, pink, or red, single or double. Flowering starts when plants are small and continues unabated until frost calls a halt. In mild-winter regions, plants will behave as the perennials they actually are.

Either in containers or in the ground, bedding begonias are excellent for mass planting. Give them good soil and regular watering. Light shade or dappled sunlight is best; plants become leggy if shade is too dense. Bronze-leafed kinds need as much light as possible to reach maximum bronziness.

BROWALLIA • Amethyst flower

If you looked only at the flower, you might think this was a small petunia—and its abundant bloom reinforces that image. The mound-shaped plant covers itself with velvet-textured flowers in bright blue, violet, or white.

Nurseries seldom offer plants, but seed specialists carry two species and selected color forms. The more common species

BROWALLIA speciosa

is *B. speciosa*, a sprawling plant with flowers to 2 inches across. Although plants can grow 1½ to 2 feet high, their spreading habit makes them good choic-

es for spilling out of containers. Compact, rather dwarf selections include 'Blue Bells Improved' and the Troll series. For a bushier plant to 2 feet high, look for *B. americana*; its flowers are only ½ inch across, but their abundance makes for an impressive color display.

Amethyst flowers revel in warmth, so they do best where summer is fairly long. Give them light shade or dappled sunlight, and water regularly. In mildest-winter areas, plants will live over winter to provide a second year of color; cut back as growth starts.

COLEUS × hybridus • Coleus

You wouldn't look twice at coleus blossoms, but the flashy foliage will catch your eye from afar. Most plants have multicolored leaves in bright or rich colors: burgundy with green edges, for example, or green with pink and brown marbling. Typical leaves are 3 to 6 inches long, broadly oval and pointed, with toothed margins. Plants may reach 2 feet in height.

Numerous strains are available, featuring extra-large or extra-narrow leaves, elaborately frilled foliage, dwarf plants, and even lax growth suitable for hanging containers. Coleus plants are branching and bushy, but repeated pinching ensures compactness. In time, blossom spikes appear at branch tips and will pro-

ANNUALS

❧

Although fewer annuals are suited to shady gardens than to sunny ones, that doesn't mean you can't achieve the sunny color impact annuals bestow. Most of the annuals described on these two pages will truly light up a shady garden with brightly colorful flowers or foliage.

duce small blue flowers; pinch out this growth to emphasize leaf production.

Plant coleus in good, organically amended soil in dappled sunlight or light shade; too much shade results in dulled or muted colors. Cuttings root easily in water or soil. Coleus plants will live over winter in mildest-winter regions; in colder areas, they can be potted and kept as house plants.

IMPATIENS wallerana • Impatiens, busy Lizzie

For masses of varied color in shade, nothing can top impatiens, pictured on page 24. The flat, circular flowers, 1 to 2 inches across, come in a dazzling array of bright colors—purple, lavender, pink, red, orange, white, and bicolor combinations. Branching, succulent stems form mound-shaped plants covered in oval, fleshy leaves. Plant breeders have developed a great assortment of flower colors and patterns (even double flowers), varied plant sizes (from 4 inches to 2 feet), and variegated foliage.

Impatiens needs well-drained, organically enriched soil and a steady supply of moisture. Grow plants in containers or in shaded borders in light to moderate shade or dappled sunlight. In frost-free climates, plants are perennial; and in mild-winter regions, volunteer seedlings may appear each year.

MIMULUS × hybridus • Monkey flower

The warm, sunny colors of monkey flower blossoms light up shaded summer gardens. Mounding, spreading plants with succulent stems and leaves produce quantities of irregularly trumpet-shaped, 2-inch blooms that may be cream, yellow, orange, red, warm pink, or brown—often spotted in a darker color. Various named strains are sold, the plants ranging up to 1½ feet high with growth lax enough to make fine plants for hanging containers.

MIMULUS × hybridus

SCHIZANTHUS pinnatus

SENECIO × hybridus

Monkey flower performs best where summer is cool to mild, in partial or light shade. Give it well-drained, highly organic soil, and water attentively.

MYOSOTIS sylvatica • Forget-me-not

Here is the lookalike annual counterpart of the perennial *Myosotis* described and pictured on page 95. This dappled-sunlight, woodland-edge plant is useful for naturalizing in the casual shady border. Bushy, foot-tall plants with fuzzy, tongue-shaped leaves produce swarms of bright true-blue blossoms in airy sprays during late winter or spring, depending on the climate. Seed catalogs offer improved strains in the classic blue as well as pink or white.

Best conditions for forget-me-not are cool to mild weather during bloom season, accompanied by regular watering. Where winter is mild, plants will live into a second year; and in all regions, plants self-sow to provide an ongoing succession of new plants to flower each year.

NICOTIANA alata • Flowering tobacco

The original flowering tobacco is a 4-foot, rather wispy plant famous for wonderfully fragrant white blossoms that open in the evening and close by day-

NICOTIANA alata 'Nicki Pink'

break. Tubular flowers flare into stars to 2 inches across, carried in clusters.

Plant breeders have produced shorter strains that bloom in pink, red, purple, and green as well as original white—some with blossoms that remain open during the day. Not all new developments, though, are scented. For the most reliable fragrance, plant 2- to 3-foot *N. a.* 'Grandiflora' or the similar species *N. sylvestris*, which grows to 5 feet.

Flowering tobacco needs only average but well-drained soil with regular watering during dry periods. Plant in dappled sunlight or light shade.

SCHIZANTHUS pinnatus • Butterfly flower

You can forgive butterfly flower its fairly short blooming period for its profusion of intricately patterned flowers. An individual blossom is funnel-shaped with lobed edge; background color may be white, pink, lavender, or violet, always with a yellow throat blotch and darker markings and veining. Plants may reach 1½ feet high, clothed in attractive but unobtrusive, fernlike foliage.

Butterfly flower is a cool-season annual. Where winter is mild and summer hot, grow it for blooms in late winter and early spring. Where summer is cool to mild—as in the Pacific Northwest—plant it for summer flowers. Grow butterfly flower in dappled sunlight or light shade in good, organically enriched soil; water regularly.

SENECIO × hybridus • Cineraria

Technically this is just a daisy; but its pulsating, fluorescent cool colors make it a daisy of exceptional character. Silky or

velvety-textured flowers may be 2 inches across, carried in broad, domed clusters over clumps of large leaves that are heart-shaped to nearly round. Flowers come in vibrant purple, violet, blue, lavender, pink, red, or white—or dark-centered with concentric bands of colors. Typical plants grow about 16 inches high, but shorter strains are available.

Cineraria excels in cool climates. In mild-winter regions, it flowers in winter and early spring; where winter is colder, spring and early summer are prime blooming times. Plants are perennial in mildest regions, and in all areas there is a tendency to self-sow if flowers are allowed to set seed. Plant in good, organically amended soil in partial or light shade; water regularly.

TORENIA fournieri • Wishbone flower

These bushy, foot-high plants give an ongoing display of flowers from summer into autumn. Inch-wide blossoms are trumpet-shaped and wide-throated—like tiny versions of florist gloxinias—revealing wishbone-shaped stamens. Basic flower color is white or light blue, usually with darker markings on the extremities.

TORENIA fournieri

Plenty of moisture and an organically-rich, well-drained soil assure success. This is a fine plant for containers as well as for the front edge of lightly shaded planting beds.

AEGOPODIUM podagraria
'Variegatum'

❧

AEGOPODIUM podagraria

Bishop's weed, gout weed
Deciduous perennial ground cover
Hardy to –30°F/–34°C
Part shade/moderate to regular water

In shade, Bishop's weed makes a lush, foot-high foliage carpet of 3-leaflet leaves resembling those of box elder *(Acer negundo)*—hence its colloquial name "ground elder." The basic species has green leaves, but the commonly planted *A. p.* 'Variegatum' has leaves irregularly edged in white. In summer, flat-topped clusters of insignificant flowers rise above the foliage on slender stems.

Culture. Nothing could be simpler to grow, given average soil, moderate watering, and some winter chill below 32°F/0°C. Vigor and a rugged constitution are Bishop's weed's strong points. In fact, it may overwhelm other plants as underground stems take over more and more space. To control the spread, install barriers of wood, concrete, or metal several inches deep into the soil.

To tidy up a frowsy planting, mow it once or twice during the growing season.

AJUGA reptans

Good companions. *Acer, Berberis, Euonymus, Ilex, Mahonia, Rhamnus, Taxus.*

❧

AJUGA reptans

Ajuga, carpet bugle
Evergreen perennial ground cover
Hardy to –30°F/–34°C
Part to full shade/regular water

Ajuga's popularity as a ground cover is easy to understand. It produces handsome low foliage in a variety of colors and sizes, plus spikes of lively blue flowers. The basic species has lustrous, dark green leaves with a quilted appearance, broadly oval and reaching 3 to 4 inches across when grown in shade. One plant will spread by runners into a solid patch of leaves, above which rise 6-inch flower spikes in spring and early summer. Named selections include some with extra-large foliage (look for 'Giant' or 'Jungle' in the name), some with bronze and purple leaves, and others with purple foliage variegated in white and pink ('Burgundy Lace') or green foliage spotted in creamy yellow ('Variegata').

Culture. Plant ajuga in average to good, well-drained soil; root rot can be a problem if soil is too moisture-retentive. Regular watering and an annual fertilizer application at the start of the growing season keep ajuga vigorous in partial or light shade.

To keep a ground cover planting tidy, mow to remove blossom stems after flowers fade.

Good companions. *Aspidistra, Camellia, ferns, Hosta, Polygonatum, Rhododendron.*

❧

AKEBIA quinata

Fiveleaf akebia
Deciduous to semi-evergreen vine
Hardy to –30°F/–34°C
Part to full shade/regular water

Though it produces unusual flowers and fruits, fiveleaf akebia is most valued for

AKEBIA quinata

its fine-textured foliage effect. Each leaf resembles a large cloverleaf, consisting of 5 oval leaflets at the end of a long leafstalk. Even a large vine in full leaf looks delicate. Vigorous, twining stems climb easily to 30 feet when supported. Clusters of dull purple flowers in spring are interesting rather than showy; the purplish, sausage-shaped (and edible) fruits that may follow are less a feature than they are curiosities.

Culture. Fiveleaf akebia is an easy, trouble-free grower given average, well-drained soil and supplemental water during dry periods. Plants may need some training during the growing season; thin and prune during the winter dormant period, before spring growth.

Good companions. *Acanthus, Anemone, Buxus, Clivia, Leucothoe, Thalictrum, Viburnum.*

❧

ALCHEMILLA mollis

Lady's mantle
Deciduous to semi-evergreen perennial
Hardy to –40°F/–40°C
Part shade/regular water

A healthy clump of lady's mantle fairly bubbles over in a symphony of green froth. Each plant grows to about 18 inches high and 2 feet across—a mound of nearly circular, scallop-edged leaves over which branched flower stems carry sprays of tiny yellow-green blossoms. Under optimum conditions, the softly hairy, grayed green leaves can reach 6 inches across; dew catches in the toothed

leaf margins and raindrops collect in leaf centers, adding sparkle.

Culture. Good soil, moist but well-drained, and atmospheric moisture bring lady's mantle to perfection. With attention to watering, plants can prosper in dry-summer regions, though they are unlikely to reach their potential luxuriance. Under best growing conditions, plants freely produce volunteer seedlings.

Good companions. *Campanula, Digitalis, Filipendula, Hosta, Polygonatum.*

ALCHEMILLA mollis

❧
AMPELOPSIS brevipedunculata

Blueberry climber
Deciduous vine
Hardy to –30°F/–34°C
Part to full shade/moderate to regular water

This relative of grape and Boston ivy (*Parthenocissus*) combines some of the best features of each. The large, 3-lobed leaves are decidedly grapelike, as is the strong growth that will attach to a support with twining tendrils. Conspicuous clusters of pea-sized fruits are white at first but change to a striking metallic blue in late summer to early autumn. At about the same time, leaves turn a brilliant red worthy of Boston ivy; in cold-winter regions, they fall from the stems, but in milder areas new leaves emerge, redden, and drop throughout winter.

For a foliage change-of-pace, look for the selection 'Elegans': this less-rampant (and somewhat less hardy) vine bears leaves variegated with white and pink.

Culture. Given average soil and just moderate watering, blueberry climber will prosper with no special attention. Prune vines as needed in winter or early spring, before new growth. Thin out excess growth in spring and summer.

Good companions. *Aucuba, Hypericum, Myrtus, Osmanthus, Podocarpus, Taxus.*

❧
ANEMONE × hybrida

Japanese anemone
Semideciduous perennial
Hardy to –20°F/–29°C
Part to full shade/regular water

During spring and summer, Japanese anemones offer foliage: trios of dark green, deeply veined, maplelike leaflets on long leafstalks. As spring progresses into summer, the foliage mass grows taller and more dense. Then, at summer's end, airy sprays of wild rose–like blossoms almost seem to float above the leaves on stems 3 to 5 feet high. White, single-flowered 'Honorine Jobert' is the most widely planted, but nurseries offer named selections in pinks as well as some with semidouble blossoms.

Although botanically distinct from *A. × hybrida*, the species *A. hupehensis, A. tomentosa,* and *A. vitifolia* are similar.

Culture. For best growth, Japanese anemones (and related species) should have good, well-drained soil that is moist

ANEMONE × hybrida

AMPELOPSIS brevipedunculata

at all times but not soggy. But even under less-than-ideal conditions—including competition from tree and shrub roots—established plants usually turn in a satisfactory display. In good soil, clumps can spread to the point of invasiveness.

Good companions. *Acer, Bergenia, Hemerocallis, Hosta, Iris foetidissima, Liriope.*

AQUILEGIA canadensis

❧
AQUILEGIA

Columbine
Deciduous perennials
Hardy to –35°F/–37°C (species);
–20°F/–29° (hybrids)
Part shade/regular water

Columbines personify delicacy and grace, from their gray-green foliage resembling maidenhair fern to their airy sprays of birdlike blossoms. Each flower has five inner petals that make a loose cup, five long and pointed petals that form a virtual saucer for the cup, and (usually) five slender spurs projecting backward from the "saucer." There are also short-spurred and spurless columbines, and some with double (and less graceful) flowers.

Retail nurseries usually sell hybrid columbines. Typical are tall (to 2½ feet), long-spurred McKana Giants and Spring Song (both mixed colors) and separate-color strains such as Crimson Star and Snow Queen. Shorter strains are Music (1½ feet) and foot-high Biedermeier and Dragonfly.

Specialty nurseries offer various species columbines, including the long-spurred, blue-and-white classic Rocky Mountain columbine, *A. caerulea*, and yellow and red *A. canadensis*. Short-spurred species (and shorter plants) include European *A. vulgaris* and *A. alpina* and Japanese *A. flabellata*. Derived from the two European columbines is the curved-spur Hensol Harebell strain, with flowers in various colors on 3-foot stems.

Culture. These mountain meadow plants can take sun only where summer is cool. In most regions, filtered or after-noon shade is best. Plant in well-drained soil of average fertility, and water regularly during dry periods. Plants play out after 3 to 5 years, but volunteer seedlings usually replace them—though their flowers may not exactly duplicate those of the parents unless you grow just one species in isolation from other columbines.

Good companions. *Campanula, ferns, Francoa, Hosta, Lamium, Platycodon, Primula.*

❧
ARBUTUS unedo

Strawberry tree
Evergreen tree, shrub
Hardy to 5°F/–15°C
Part shade/little to moderate water

Tree or shrub depends on what you start with and how long you wait. The basic species is shrubby for years but eventual-ly rises (unless deliberately restricted) as a multitrunked tree. Several small-grow-ing selections stay shrubby permanently.

ARBUTUS unedo

This is a handsome plant in all sea-sons. Dark green, semiglossy, 3-inch oval leaves form a dense foliage cover throughout the year; young stems and leaf petioles are rhubarb red. In autumn and early winter, drooping clusters of small, urn-shaped white flowers decorate the plant—coincident with the ripening of strawberry-size yellow to red fruits from the previous year's flowers. Older stems develop shaggy, red-brown bark.

Selections that stay shrubby include 'Compacta' (to about 10 feet high) and pink-flowered 'Oktoberfest' (6 to 8 feet tall). 'Elfin King' grows only to about 5 feet and bears flowers and fruit all year.

Culture. Strawberry tree is remarkably adaptable. Give it well-drained soil and routine watering until it is established. After that, it will thrive with regular gar-den watering or even little or no supple-mental moisture (except in the desert).

Good companions. *Aegopodium, Bergenia, Hedera, Juniperus, Myrtus, Rhamnus, Rubus.*

❧
ARDISIA

Ardisia
Evergreen shrubs
Hardiness varies
Full shade/frequent water

Marlberry, *A japonica,* spreads by under-ground stems and grows no higher than 1½ feet, making a fine ground cover in a moist, shady garden where temperatures remain above 10°F/–12°C. Leathery, bright green 4-inch leaves cluster toward the tips of branches growing vertically from the soil. Insignificant white flowers appear in autumn, forming bright red

berries that last into winter. With some searching, you may find selections with white- or yellow-variegated leaves.

Red berries and lustrous leaves also characterize coralberry, *A. crenata,* but plants are upright to 4 to 6 feet and hardy only to about 25°F/–4°C.

Culture. Both species thrive in an organically enriched soil that is kept moist. For a marlberry ground cover, set plants about 18 inches apart. Prune only to even up the foliage height.

Good companions. *Clethra, Cornus, Franklinia, Stewartia, Thalictrum.*

❧
ARUNCUS dioicus

Goatsbeard
Deciduous perennial
Hardy to –35°F/–37°C
Part to full shade/regular to
frequent water

Although goatsbeard is a perennial, an established plant bulks up enough to function as a shrub. Great clumps of broad, fernlike leaves form 4-foot-high mounds, above which feathery plumes of creamy white flowers rise in summer. If that seems too massive, look for the selection 'Kneiffii'; its plumes top out at about 3 feet, above filagree-fine foliage.

Culture. With its preference for moist soil, you can even plant goatsbeard in poorly-drained soil . It's a perfect candi-date for the ever-moist soil beside a pond, yet it also will thrive in retentive soil with ordinary garden watering. Atmospheric moisture is another requi-site; plants fall short of their potential where summer is hot and dry.

Good companions. *Filipendula, Hy-drangea, Ligularia, Thalictrum, Trollius.*

ARDISIA crenata

ENCYCLOPEDIA OF SHADE PLANTS

ARUNCUS dioicus

ASPIDISTRA elatior

❧ ASARUM

Wild ginger
Deciduous and evergreen perennials
Hardiness varies
Full shade/regular to frequent water

Wild gingers have far-flung origins—Canada, western and eastern United States, and Europe—but they all share a general pattern. Plants grow from slowly spreading rootstocks, with leafstalks rising to bear shiny, rubbery leaves, heart-shaped to nearly circular. Inconspicuous purplish flowers bloom at ground level.

Evergreen *A. caudatum,* from the Pacific Coast, is hardy to around 0°F/–18°C. Dark green leaves 2 to 7 inches across are carried 7 to 10 inches above the soil. European wild ginger, *A. europaeum,* also is evergreen but will grow where winter lows reach –20°F/–29°C. Its 3-inch leaves grow on stalks to 6 inches long. Deciduous *A. canadense* is the hardiest (to –40°F/–40°C) and the tallest, with 6-inch leaves on foot-long stalks.

Culture. In organically enriched soil with plenty of moisture, wild gingers will spread enthusiastically into lush carpets

ASARUM caudatum

of overlapping leaves. Use them as small-scale ground covers among taller perennials, beneath shrubs and trees, and along paths.

Good companions. *Camellia, Cornus, Enkianthus, ferns, Hosta, Polygonatum.*

❧ ASPIDISTRA elatior

Aspidistra, cast-iron plant
Evergreen perennial
Hardy to 5°F/–15°C
Part to full shade/moderate to regular water

This familiar, indestructible house plant—famous for thriving with little light and water—is a striking garden ornament in any degree of shade. Gradually expanding clumps contain numerous elliptical to lance-shaped leaves up to 2½ feet long and 4 inches wide, each supported by a 6- to 8-inch stalk. Leaves are tough but flexible (their texture somewhat like oilcloth), typically dark green. Variegated forms (one spotted, others striped) are sometimes offered in nurseries.

Culture. For best appearance, give aspidistra organically enriched, well-drained soil. This plant's drought tolerance is legendary, but moderate to routine watering produces the best-looking specimens. Striped forms tend to lose their variegation if grown in especially rich soil or fertilized heavily.

Good companions. *Ajuga, Anemone, Bergenia, Epimedium, Helleborus, Lamium, Viola.*

❧ ASTILBE

Astilbe, false spiraea, meadow sweet
Deciduous perennials
Hardy to –25°F/–32°C
Part shade/regular water

Wherever summer is humid but not extremely hot, astilbes will furnish plenty of summer color in white, pink, or red over clumps of handsome foliage.

ASPIDISTRA elatior

Individual flowers are tiny, but they are carried in impressive, feathery plumes to great effect. Some species have vertical floral plumes, and others are more horizontally branched and arching or drooping at the tips. All have fairly low clumps of much-divided, fernlike foliage. Leafy flower stalks grow from 6 inches to 5 feet tall, depending on the species or named selection.

Most available astilbes fall into the 2- to 4-foot height range, many of them *A. × arendsii* hybrids. Several have red flowers over bronzy leaves; worth special mention is *A. taquetii* 'Superba', a magenta-colored, late-flowering selection that tolerates more heat and dryness than most. For the

ASTILBE × arendsii 'Peach Blossom'

front of the border, look for 18-inch *A. chinensis* 'Finale' (light pink) and two 12-inch selections: *A. chinensis* 'Pumila' (a spreading plant with rosy lilac flowers, good for small-scale ground cover) and *A. simplicifolia* 'Sprite' (pink flowers, bronze leaves).

Culture. For success with astilbes, give them good soil enriched with plenty of organic matter, and then make sure they get plenty of moisture but not so much that soil becomes waterlogged. Clumps

ASTRANTIA major

will need dividing every 4 or 5 years in spring.

Good companions. *Asarum, Bergenia, Galax, Hosta, Prunella, Trollius.*

❧
ASTRANTIA

Masterwort
Deciduous perennials
Hardy to –10°F/–23°C
Part shade/regular water

Charming rather than flashy, masterworts provide pastel summer color for lightly shaded gardens. Long-stalked, deeply lobed leaves about 6 inches across grow in clumps. In the most common species, *A. major,* slender 2½-foot stems branch at the top in airy floral sprays. What appears to be a pincushionlike individual flower is really a grouping of small flowers surrounded by a "ruff" of pointed, papery bracts. Greenish white bracts and white to pinkish flowers are typical, but all-white and pink selections exist. *A. maxima* is similar, with slightly larger pink flowers and more conspicuous bracts.

Culture. Plant in good soil, organically enriched, and make sure masterworts have a steady supply of moisture during the growing season. Volunteer seedlings will appear if you don't remove spent flower heads.

Good companions. *Ferns, Heucherella, Hosta, Platycodon, Pulmonaria, Tiarella.*

❧
AUCUBA japonica

Japanese aucuba
Evergreen shrub
Hardy to 0°F/–18°C
Part to full shade/moderate to regular water

Japanese aucuba is a time-tested solution to the problem of shade combined with dryness. With some attention to soil and watering, it rises above the purely utilitarian to become a shrub of considerable beauty.

The basic species is a solid, bulky plant growing to 10 feet high and wide, densely covered in glossy, leathery, dark green leaves—toothed ovals to 8 inches long. Inconspicuous little maroon flowers appear in winter; female plants then produce berries that ripen to red the next autumn if there's a male pollinator nearby.

Named selections, many with variegated leaves (mostly female plants), are the usual nursery offerings. These range from yellow-edged to yellow-centered to the widely sold 'Variegata'—which looks like a drop cloth for a yellow painting project. 'Fructo Albo' has white-variegated leaves and pinkish buff fruits; 'Crotonifolia', a male, offers variegation in yellow and white. In all-green foliage, you also have the female plants 'Longifolia' ('Salicifolia'), with narrow, willow-like leaves, and 'Nana', a 3-foot-high version of the basic species.

Culture. You can grow Japanese aucuba in a broad range of soils, but in sandy and heavy soils you'll get better performance with organic amendment. Established plants need moderate or little watering and can hold their own with tree roots.

AUCUBA japonica

AZARA dentata

Good companions. *Epimedium, ferns, Hydrangea, Podocarpus, Rubus, Viburnum, Vancouveria.*

❧
AZARA

Azara
Evergreen shrubs
Hardiness varies
Part shade/regular water

These shrub-trees with dark green, box-woodlike leaves becomes more interesting and graceful as they age and grow.

Boxleaf azara, *A. microphylla*, grows to 18 feet with a 12-foot spread. Branches grow in fanlike sprays, making this a natural for espalier training. Short clusters of small yellow flowers in late winter exude a sweet scent reminiscent of vanilla. Plants are hardy to 5°F/–15°C. Less hardy *A. dentata* (to about 25°F/ –4°C) grows as a dense 15-foot shrub-tree good for hedge planting.

Culture. Plant azaras either where they will get morning sun and afternoon shade or where there's light or dappled shade all day. Give them average to good soil, well-drained, and water during dry periods.

Good companions. *Acanthus, Aucuba, Hypericum, Leucothoe, Rhododendron.*

BULBS

ENDYMION hispanicus

❧

Before deciduous trees put on their yearly mantle of new leaves, the sunny ground beneath their branches can host a variety of flowering bulbs. Except as noted, the following bulbs prefer regular watering from when growth begins until foliage yellows in mid- to late spring, then little or no water once foliage dies down.

CROCUS • Crocus • Corm

Hardy to –40°F/-40°C. Chalicelike flowers in jewel tones sparkle close to the ground in late winter and early spring. Plant 2 to 3 inches deep in well-drained soil; corms can take summer water if drainage is good. Performance is best where winters go below freezing.

ENDYMION • Bluebell • Bulb

Hardy to –30°F/–35°C. Stems bearing bell-shaped blossoms spring up from clumps of straplike leaves. Spanish bluebell, *E. hispanicus,* reaches 20 inches; English bluebell, *E. non-scriptus,* grows to 12 inches. Both are available in blue, white, and pink. English bluebell needs subfreezing winters. Plant 3 inches deep in average soil.

ERANTHIS • Winter aconite • Tuber

Hardy to –10°F/–23°C. Bright yellow, buttercuplike flowers can hardly wait to bloom, often appearing through the snow. Flowers set on leafy collars top bare stems 2 to 8 inches tall; lobed leaves come later. Plant 3 inches deep in well-drained, organically-enriched soil. Plants need subfreezing winter temperatures.

GALANTHUS • Snowdrop • Bulb

Hardy to –40°F/–40°C. This harbinger of spring features strap-shaped leaves and slender stems bearing single bell-shaped white flowers with green markings. Common snowdrop, *G. nivalis,* grows 6 to 9 inches high; giant snowdrop, *G. elwesii,* makes it to 12 inches. Both need subfreezing winter temperatures for good performance; choose giant snowdrop where winter chill is slight. Plant 3 to 4 inches deep, and water all year.

LEUCOJUM • Snowflake • Bulb

Hardy to –30°F/–35°C. Often incorrectly called snowdrops *(Galanthus),* snow-flakes are taller and have more symmetrical blossoms—and one species bears several per stem. Summer snowflake, *L. aestivum,* carries 3 to 5 flowers on its 1½-foot stems. It's the choice for mild-winter climates, where it can bloom in late autumn. Foot-tall spring snowflake, *L. vernum,* needs some winter chill. Plant 3 inches deep; summer snowflake grows in varied soils, but spring snowflake needs good soil and plenty of moisture. Both need some water in summer.

MUSCARI • Grape hyacinth • Bulb

Hardy to –40°F/–40°C. Low clumps of grasslike leaves send up stems topped by tight blossom spikes that look like bunches of miniature grapes. Most widely grown is 8-inch *M. armeniacum,* available in blue and white forms. Italian grape hyacinth, *M. botryoides,* may reach 12 inches. Plant both 2 inches deep in well-drained soil.

NARCISSUS • Daffodil, jonquil, narcissus • Bulb

Most hardy to –30°F/–35°C. The characteristic flowers—cups or tubes set on petal ruffs—occur singly or in small clusters atop hollow stems. Yellow is the main color, but there are all-white flowers and orange, red, and pink combinations. Species and hybrids range from less than 6 inches high to flashy "giants" on 2-foot stems. Tazetta types, including paper-white narcissus, are hardy only to about 10°F/–12°C. Plant 3 to 6 inches deep, depending on bulb size; they can take summer water.

SCILLA • Squill, bluebell • Bulb

Most hardy to –30°/–35°C. Three squills are among the earliest spring flowers, their bell- or star-shaped blossoms rising from clumps of strap-shaped leaves. The early-bloomers (which need subfreezing winter temperature) are *S. bifolia, S. siberica* (Siberian squill), and *S. tubergeniana,* all under a foot tall. Blue is common to all; the first two also come in white, pink, and violet. Spring-flowering *S. peruviana* or Peruvian scilla (actually a Mediterranean native) needs no winter chill and is hardy just to 20°F/–7°C. Its 12-inch stems carry large clusters of violet-blue blossoms.

Plant Peruvian scilla 4 inches deep, all others 2 inches deep. All tolerate some summer watering in well-drained soil.

TULIPA • Tulip • Bulb

Hardy to –40°F/–40°C. Tulips offer a rainbow of colors in chalice-shaped blossoms. Sizes and shapes vary widely, from 6-inch species with narrow petals to elegant, 3-foot aristocrats. There are even double-flowered tulips that look like peonies. Plant 2½ times as deep as bulb width in good, well-drained soil. All need subfreezing winter temperature to bloom from year to year.

BEGONIA × tuberhybrida

❧ BEGONIA × *tuberhybrida*

Tuberous begonia
Deciduous tuberous perennial
Tender
Part to full shade/regular water

This wonderfully varied group of plants includes the familiar bedding begonias (see page 60), various shrubby and cane-stem types, and the elaborately patterned rex begonias usually seen as house plants. All are candidates for the shade garden during warmer months. But the magnificent summer blossoms of tuberous begonias make them the star of the group.

A well-grown tuberous begonia may grow 1½ feet high and produce saucer-size blooms that mimic camellias, carnations, and roses. Colors include red, orange, yellow, pink, cream, and white—sometimes edged in a contrasting color. Thick, fleshy, upright stems support irregularly shaped, pointed leaves that grow to 8 inches long. Leaves all point one direction, and flowers face the same way. Hanging basket types have drooping stems and a profusion of smaller, downward-facing flowers.

Culture. Success with tuberous begonias begins with climate. They need moist air and moderate temperatures—neither too cool nor too warm, preferably with nighttime temperature above 60°F/16°C. Regionally, this includes the Pacific and North Atlantic coasts, Great Lakes coastal areas, and northern Minnesota and Michigan.

For the longest bloom season, start tubers indoors 6 to 8 weeks before the outdoor planting time—when the overnight low temperature won't go below 50°F/10°C. When sprouted tubers have two leaves (or plants are 3 inches high), repot each in an 8- to 10-inch pot in a fast-draining, largely-organic potting medium. To grow in the ground, liberally amend soil with organic matter before setting out the young plants. Either way, give plants filtered sunlight or light shade. Fertilize lightly every 2 weeks for the best and most blooms.

When flower production tapers off in late summer or early autumn, stop fertilizing and cut back on water (give just enough to prevent wilting). When leaves start to yellow, stop watering. Dig or unpot tubers when stems separate easily from tubers; shake off soil, dry tubers in the sun for 3 days, then place in a single layer in a shallow box and cover with sand, sawdust, peat moss, or vermiculite. Store in a cool place (preferably 40° to 50°F/4° to 10°C) until planting time the following year.

Good companions. *Asarum, Aspidistra, ferns, Hosta, Lamium, Polygonatum, Tiarella.*

❧ BERBERIS

Barberry
Deciduous and evergreen shrubs
Hardiness varies
Part shade/moderate to regular water

Spiny-stemmed barberries are supremely utilitarian barrier plants, but they get high marks for garden ornament, too. Most are fine-textured with small leaves (spiny-edged in some species); deciduous kinds provide yellow to red autumn color. Individual flowers (usually yellow) are small but often plentiful enough to be a real spectacle. Small berries come later—generally red, dark blue, or black—and remain decorative through winter.

Availability varies by region, and a few species are forbidden in grain-growing areas because they are a host for black rust in wheat. The following is a sampling of the more popular species.

Among evergreens, the Darwin barberry, *B. darwinii,* is a standout for its foliage-obscuring display of orange-yellow flowers and later dark blue berries. Fountain-like growth can reach 10 feet high and 7 feet wide, the arching stems covered in hollylike, inch-long leaves. Plants are hardy to 10°F/–12°C. Warty barberry, *B. verruculosa,* takes temperatures to 0°F/–18°C. Plants become 4-foot mounds of inch-long, spiny dark green leaves with white undersides. In cold weather, plants are spangled with bits of color as some leaves turn red. Yellow spring blossoms lead to violet berries in autumn.

Deciduous species include the ever-popular Japanese barberry, *B. thunbergii,* and its variants, mostly hardy to –20°F/ –29°C. The basic species consists of arching stems 4 to 6 feet high and wide, covered with nearly round, 1½-inch leaves. Deep green in spring and summer, they become a mixture of yellow, orange, and red in autumn. Stems then are decorated with suspended red berries that last into winter. The selection 'Sparkle' is slightly smaller, its leaves especially vivid in autumn. The best-known selection with colored foliage is *B. t.* 'Atropurpurea', red-leaf Japanese barberry; the burgundy red of sun-grown plants is subdued to

BERBERIS thunbergii

bronze or purple-infused green in shade. 'Crimson Pygmy' ('Atropurpurea Nana'), hardy to –10°F/–23°C, makes a 2-foot-high bronzed red mound; 'Cherry Bomb' is similar but about twice as big. 'Kobold' offers bright green foliage on a 2-foot plant; 'Aurea' is the same size but has yellow leaves.

Culture. Tough and adaptable, barberries will grow in rich or poor soil, in prairie heat or northwestern coolness, with little or ordinary garden watering. Thin out plants periodically to remove dead and twiggy stems and to encourage strong renewal growth.

Good companions. *Bergenia, Euonymus, Hemerocallis, Juniperus, Taxus, Vancouveria.*

BERGENIA

Bergenia
Evergreen and deciduous perennials
Hardiness varies
Part to full shade/moderate
to regular water

Handsome foliage is reason enough to plant bergenias; attractive flowers are an almost unnecessary bonus! Leaves are oval to nearly round and up to a foot long on equally long stalks. Their texture is leathery, the surface deeply veined—smooth and glossy on most, but covered with hairs in one. Cold weather often brings out bronzy purple tints. Each plant makes an informal foliage rosette; thick, creeping rootstocks form gradually expanding clumps. In winter or early spring, dense spikes of bell-shaped flowers appear among or above the leaves.

Winter-blooming bergenia, *B. crassifolia,* is a West Coast favorite, evergreen but still hardy to –30°F/–34°C. Lilac to rosy purple flowers appear above the wavy-edged, rubbery leaves. The similar and equally cold-tolerant heartleaf bergenia, *B. cordifolia,* waits until spring to produce dark pink blossoms among its glossy leaves. Deciduous *B. ciliata,* hardy to –10°F/–23°C, has silky-haired leaves

BERGENIA cordifolia

that emerge bronze in spring along with light pink to white flowers. Specialty nurseries offer named hybrids (such as 'Abendglut' and 'Bressingham White') similar to *B. crassifolia* and *B. cordifolia,* with flowers in magenta to pink to white.

Culture. It's easy to relegate these plants to deep shade and dry soil simply because they'll grow there. But their true beauty shines when you give them average or good soil with some organic enrichment and at least moderate watering.

Good companions. *Anemone, Astilbe, Brunnera, Digitalis, Polygonatum, Thalictrum.*

BLETILLA striata

Chinese ground orchid
Deciduous perennial
Hardy to 10°F/–12°C (with protection)
Part shade/regular water

An established clump of Chinese ground orchid is a certain conversation piece. From a drift of light green, elongated, pleated leaves rise branched, 1½- to 2-foot stems bearing perfect scaled-down replicas of florist-shop cattleya orchids. The basic color of these 2-inch flowers is a typical orchid lavender, but for contrast you can plant the white-flowered form 'Alba'. Bloom lasts more than a month, beginning in mid- to late spring.

BLETILLA striata

Culture. This woodland orchid revels in organically enriched soil with a steady moisture supply from the onset of growth through the flowering period. Where winter low temperatures reach 20°F/–7°C or lower, cover the planting area with straw or evergreen boughs to keep the tuberous roots from freezing.

Good companions. *Asarum, Corydalis, Dicentra, ferns, Hosta, Lamium, Pulmonaria.*

BRUNNERA macrophylla

Brunnera, Siberian bugloss
Deciduous perennial
Hardy to –35°F/–37°C
Part shade/regular water

Brunnera's foliage and flowers present an appealing contrast. Heart-shaped, 4-inch leaves form solid low mounds in early spring. Above this mass of foliage rise threadlike stems bearing airy clusters of vivid blue, ¼-inch

BRUNNERA macrophylla

flowers that show the relationship to forget-me-not *(Myosotis).* As the growing season continues, leaves get bigger and stems rise higher—to 2 feet by the time flowering ceases. Plant clumps remain fresh-looking until frost.

The creamy white–marked leaves of *B. m.* 'Variegata' are particularly good for lighting up the shady garden.

Culture For best appearance, give brunnera fairly good, organically amended soil and ordinary garden watering (though plants will survive with even moderate watering). Growth is easy in light shade,

BUXUS sempervirens

filtered sunlight, or morning sunlight with afternoon shade. This is a fine plant for naturalizing in drifts in front of shrubs and larger perennials; volunteer seedlings make this easy to accomplish.

Good companions. *Bergenia, Camellia, Doronicum, Hosta, Lilium, Polygonatum, Thalictrum.*

❧

BUXUS

Boxwood
Evergreen shrubs
Hardiness varies
Part shade/regular water

Mention boxwood, and the word "hedge" comes to mind. These are neat, small-leafed shrubs that can be clipped into precise ribbons of green—or just as easily sculpted into fanciful topiary shapes. Left to its own devices, though, a boxwood develops into a surprisingly billowy, bulky, attractive plant.

Japanese boxwood, *B. microphylla japonica,* is hardy to 0°F/–18°C and is the best choice where summers are dry or soil is alkaline. Leaves are round-tipped, no more than an inch long; bright green in summer, they become bronzed over winter in many areas. Unpruned plants grow 4 to 6 feet in all directions, but plants can be clipped to less than a foot high. The selection 'Richardii' is faster-growing and potentially larger (if untrimmed). 'Compacta' is particularly small, slow-growing, and tiny-leafed. Two hardier selections are 'Winter Gem' (to –15F°/–26°C) and 'Green Beauty' (to –10°F/–23°C), which maintains its green leaves in winter.

Korean boxwood, *B. microphylla koreana,* is hardy to –18°F/–28°C. This plant is shorter, smaller-leafed, and slower growing than Japanese boxwood. In California, a plant sold as Korean boxwood and labeled *B. harlandii* is neither that species nor true Korean boxwood. Still, it's a good boxwood for hot-summer regions; cold tolerance is to 0°F/–18°C.

Common boxwood, *B. sempervirens,* is hardy to –10°F/–23°C. This is the boxwood you'll find in colonial Williamsburg and in formal European gardens. Where summers are cool to mild and soil is neutral to acid, this is the one to grow. Old, untrimmed plants may become mounds 20 feet high and wide, solid masses of glossy, dark green leaves 1¼ inches long. Many named selections exist, differing in growth habit or rate, foliage size, and leaf color—including yellow or white variegations.

Culture. For best growth and appearance, give boxwoods average to good soil and regular watering. In cool- or mild-summer regions, established plants can endure neglect at some sacrifice of looks.

Good companions. *Camellia, Enkianthus, Hydrangea, Kalmia, Nandina, Pieris, Rhododendron.*

❧

CALADIUM bicolor

Caladium, fancy-leafed caladium
Deciduous tuberous perennial
Tender
Part to full shade/regular to frequent water

CALADIUM bicolor 'Fannie Munson'

Few plants offer such colorful, varied, and truly eye-catching foliage. Trot out the adjectives—"flamboyant," "gaudy," "tropical," and "peacocklike" all apply.

From each tuber grow numerous slim stalks, each supporting a thin-textured leaf shaped like an elongated heart. Well-grown plants may reach 2 to 3 feet tall with leaves up to 1 foot wide and 1½ feet long, in a range of color arrangements that can include veining, dotting, splashing, washing, and edging.

Culture. Caladiums revel in heat and humidity, hence their popularity in Florida and Gulf Coast areas. They also need rich, organically amended soil; plenty of water; and plenty of light but not direct sun. Where climate is to their liking, caladiums will easily grow in garden beds. Elsewhere, container culture is more reliable.

For garden planting, choose a spot that gets filtered sunlight or plenty of light but no direct sun. Before planting, liberally enrich the soil with organic matter, such as leaf mold, compost, peat moss, or ground bark.

Set out nursery plants so that tuber tops are even with the soil surface. Keep soil moist, and increase watering as more leaves develop. Mist daily; apply half-strength liquid fertilizer every other week. Remove any flowers (like small callas) so plant energy stays focused on leaf production. When leaves begin to yellow and die down in late summer or early autumn, decrease watering. After all leaves have yellowed, dig up tubers and store them as for *Begonia* (see page 68).

For container planting, start tubers indoors a month before outside temperatures will reach 70°F/21°C. Follow the container-culture directions for *Begonia* on page 68.

Good companions. *Clivia, ferns, Hemerocallis, Hosta, Liriope/Ophiopogon.*

CAMELLIA japonica

ᴣᴇ

CAMELLIA

Camellia
Evergreen shrubs
Hardy to 10°F/–12°C except as noted
Part to full shade/regular water

Within their hardiness range, camellias have everything in their favor. They bear lovely blossoms on plants noted for handsome foliage; they flower mostly from late autumn to early spring when little else does; and they are quite easy to grow.

Typical camellia foliage is dark green and glossy, each leaf a pointed oval. Camellias sold in nurseries are of several distinct types. Japonica, sasanqua/ hiemalis, and reticulata types reflect the species responsible for the named selections in the grouping. All the "japonicas," for example, are largely derived from *C. japonica.* A fourth category is the catchall "hybrid camellias": plants derived from two or more species.

Japonica camellias are by far the largest category—the plants that come to mind when you hear the word "camellia." Flowers may be white, pink, red, or variegated combinations; size is 2 to 7 inches across, ranging from a single row of petals to double with a rosebud center. Named selections vary in size, plant habit, and rate of growth; some may reach 20 feet tall in time, though 6 to 12 feet is more common.

Reticulata camellias have the largest (to 9 inches across), most breathtakingly

beautiful flowers, with silken petals in red, pinks, and variegated combinations. Plants are generally larger and more tree-like than the typical japonica; they also are more open and rangy, with duller foliage and less of it.

Sasanqua/hiemalis camellias are a bit hardier—to 5°F/–15°C. Most nurseries sell their named selections as "sasanquas." In general, these have dark green, glossy leaves that are smaller and narrower than those of japonicas. Some plants are upright and bushy, others limber or nearly vinelike. The earliest-flowering start blooming along with autumn chrysanthemums; even later-blooming sasanquas are mostly finished by midwinter. Sasanquas have smaller and shorter-lived flowers than most japonicas, but far more of them. They are good for mass planting (even as hedges); the most vinelike can be planted as ground covers.

Hybrid camellias may derive from japonicas, reticulatas, sasanquas, and lesser-known species. Some have been developed for cold-tolerance. Japonica-reticulata hybrids are attempts to wed the reticulata flower with the handsome japonica plant. Some of the best known hybrids are from japonicas crossed with *C. saluenensis.* Referred to as *C.* × *williamsii,* these produce great quantities of flowers on graceful, adaptable plants.

Culture. For best results, plant where light will be good but direct sunlight will be filtered through trees or lath. In cool-to mild-summer regions, morning sun followed by afternoon shade is satisfactory. Give plants well-drained soil liberally enriched with organic matter. Plant with the juncture of roots and trunk a bit above soil grade, and mulch to maintain coolness.

Well-established plants can be fairly tolerant of dry periods, but best growth and appearance come with regular watering during dry periods.

Good companions. *Acer, Asarum, Bergenia, Buxus, Epimedium, Helleborus, Ilex, Rhododendron.*

ᴣᴇ

CAMPANULA

Bellflower
Deciduous and evergreen perennials
Hardy to –30°F/–34°C except as noted
Part shade/regular water

Bellflowers have a Victorian cottage-garden charm, a wildflowerlike delicacy that belies toughness. The species described here exhibit the spread of possibilities, from upright-stemmed, deciduous clumps to evergreen ground covers.

Clustered bellflower, *C. glomerata,* has clumps of broad, wavy-edged leaves from which leafy 1- to 2-foot stems rise, bearing tight clusters of flaring, upward-facing bells in late spring and summer. The standard color is blue-violet, but named selections offer more colors (including white) and heights.

Tall *C. lactiflora* (hardy to –10°F/ –23°C) carries phloxlike domed clusters of open-faced, starry bells atop 3- to 5-foot stems liberally clothed in pointed 3-inch leaves. Flowers may be blue, white, or pink. Pale blue 'Pouffe' makes a mound of flowers barely over a foot tall.

Two ground cover species come from the Balkans. Serbian bellflower, *C. poscharskyana,* is vigorous nearly to the point of being weedy. Its clumps of heart-shaped leaves spread by rooting runners to form solid foliage carpets. Semi-upright stems appear in late spring, bearing starry, soft blue bells; a white-flowered form also is available. Dalmatian bellflower, *C. portenschlagiana* (often sold as *C. muralis*), is hardy to –20°F/–29°C. It resembles a more diminutive Serbian bellflower with less rampant spread. From late spring to midsummer, plants are covered in small

(Continued on page 74)

CAMPANULA portenschlagiana

ADIANTUM aleuticum

ADIANTUM • Maidenhair fern

Hardiness varies. Plants form gradually spreading clumps of needle-thin black stems. Two similar species have twice-pinnate fronds with fan-shaped leaflets producing a lacy effect; both are hardy to about 5°F/–15°C. Southern maidenhair, *A. capillus-veneris,* is the most familiar maidenhair fern; established clumps reach 1½ feet high. California maidenhair, *A. jordanii,* is just for West Coast gardens, where it grows to 2 feet tall.

Five-finger or Western maidenhair fern, *A. aleuticum* (formerly *A. pedatum*), is hardy to –30°F/–34°C. It can reach 2½ feet high under best conditions, a mass of overlapping fronds that give the appearance of being palmate.

Grow maidenhair ferns in light to medium shade and well-drained, organically enriched soil. Southern maidenhair and five-finger fern must be watered regularly; California maidenhair—suitable only for its native western area and sometimes difficult even there—will take some dryness. All species die back to the ground in hard frosts.

ATHYRIUM nipponicum 'Pictum'

FERNS

❧

Shade and ferns are a natural combination. In the wild, most ferns grow in shade of one sort or another—light to deep, moist to dry, warm to cool.

Fern leaves are known as "fronds," and nearly all are constructed in one of two ways. *Pinnate* fronds are featherlike: a long central axis bears leaflets on either side *(once-pinnate),* produces secondary axes that bear leaflets *(twice-pinnate),* or is even further divided the same way. *Palmate* fronds are built like an outstreched hand, with multiple "fingers" (each bearing leaflets) radiating from a central point.

ATHYRIUM

Hardy to –35°F/–37°C. These are deciduous ferns of great delicacy and easy culture. Most widely grown is lady fern, *A. filix-femina,* which produces twice-pinnate fronds 3 to 4 feet long or more in a shuttlecock-shaped clump. In time, plants spread by thick rhizomes into fairly loose clumps. Fern specialists carry numerous selected forms with more elaborately constructed fronds.

Japanese painted fern, *A. nipponicum* 'Pictum' (formerly *A. goeringianum* 'Pictum'), produces 1½-foot-long, twice-pinnate fronds that have dark red midribs and vary in color from purplish green at the base to silvery gray-green at the tips. Clumps are more compact than those of lady fern.

Both species prefer acid soil, moist and organically amended, and a reliable moisture supply. Best performance is in light to moderate shade in a climate offering some humidity, cool or warm.

BLECHNUM spicant • Deer fern

Hardy to –35°F/–37°C. Two types of fronds give deer fern a special character. Sterile evergreen fronds are pinnate, about 1½ inches

BLECHNUM spicant

across at the widest point, their glossy green leaflets closely spaced. These arch to about 1½ feet high. From the center of the clump of sterile fronds rise fertile fronds: upright and very narrow, with widely spaced leaflets.

Given a constantly moist, organically enriched soil, deer fern will grow in moderate to deep shade. It's a good choice for planting beneath leggy shrubs and small trees where light is limited.

DRYOPTERIS • Wood fern

Hardy to 0°F/–18°C. Spreading wood fern, *D. expansa,* forms lush clumps of elaborately pinnate, arching fronds to 3 feet long—dark green in color and triangular in outline. (See photo on page 34.) You may find this plant sold under the name *D. dilatata.*

Japanese shield fern, *D. erythrosora,* has twice-pinnate fronds about 1½ feet long and half as wide. The fronds are coppery red when young, maturing to dark green.

Wood ferns are easy growers in partial to complete shade, given organically enriched soil and a regular moisture supply.

MATTEUCCIA struthiopteris • Ostrich fern

Hardy to –50°F/–46°C. Shuttlecock-shaped clumps consist of yellowish green to dark green pinnate fronds. In cool, moist regions, fronds may grow 6 feet long; in dryer climates and where the growing season is short, plants are shorter. In all climates, fronds die down in autumn. Plants spread by underground rhizomes to form colonies.

Nurseries sometimes sell a fern labeled *M. pensylvanica.* This is actually a North American native form of *M. struthiopteris* and is now considered to be the same species.

MATTEUCCIA struthiopteris

Ostrich fern grows best in good soil with plenty of water. Give it dappled sunlight to moderate shade.

NEPHROLEPIS cordifolia • Southern sword fern

Hardy to 20°F/–7°C. Narrow, pinnate fronds reach 2 to 3 feet high, the clumps spreading by fuzzy, wiry runners to become thick colonies of evergreen foliage.

This is one of the easiest ferns to grow, succeeding even in desert climates. It will take dense shade, erratic watering, and poor soil—though it looks better when it is grown in average to good soil, well-drained, and watered whenever the soil surface becomes dry.

OSMUNDA regalis • Royal fern

Hardy to –30°F/–34°C. For size alone, this fern rates the name "royal." Twice-

OSMUNDA regalis

pinnate fronds grow upward and outward to a height of 6 feet, forming impressive fountainlike clumps. Fronds die down in autumn, turning golden in the process. Many fibrous roots show at the bases of clumps—the "osmunda fiber" once used as a growing medium for many orchids.

Plenty of water is a key ingredient to success with royal fern; it will prosper at margins of ponds and streams where soil actually is boglike. Give it partial to full shade.

PHYLLITIS scolopendrium • Hart's tongue fern

Hardy to –30°F/–34°C. Like other ferns, this one forms clumps of upright fronds. What sets it apart is that its narrow, 9- to 18-inch fronds are strap-shaped rather than divided into leaflets. Clumps remain compact, only slowly increasing in diameter. Some nurseries may now sell this fern under its recently reclassified name *Asplenium scolopendrium.*

Hart's tongue fern prefers always-moist soil and woodland conditions—

PHYLLITIS scolopendrium

partial to full shade, with soil somewhat acid to slightly alkaline. Appearance suffers where summer is hot and dry.

POLYSTICHUM

POLYSTICHUM munitum

Hardy to –5°F/–21°C. Evergreen sword fern, *P. munitum,* forms handsome, dense clumps of arching fronds. Pinnate fronds containing leathery, glossy dark green leaflets grow 1 to 4 feet long, depending on garden conditions. This fern is particularly successful in its native western North America. Christmas fern, *P. acrostichoides,* is the eastern North American counterpart in general appearance, though its fronds grow only about 2 feet long and its leaflets aren't glossy.

The soft-shield fern, *P. setiferum,* makes arching-spreading clumps of soft green, lacelike twice-pinnate fronds. Selections with more elaborately constructed foliage are sold by fern specialists. Similar Japanese lace fern, *P. polyblepharum,* is taller and more upright.

All the *Polystichum* species prefer well-drained, organically amended soil and full shade. Sword fern will thrive with just moderate water, once established, but the others need moisture at all times.

WOODWARDIA fimbriata • Giant chain fern

Hardy to 0°F/–18°C. Here is a fern that makes a definite statement. (See photo on page 33). Where it is native, in Pacific Coast forests, its twice-pinnate fronds can grow 9 feet high. The arching-spreading clumps manage to be both massive and graceful.

Locate giant chain fern in dappled sunlight, partial shade, or full shade (light to deep). Best growth comes with plenty of water, humidity, and organically rich soil, but established clumps can withstand some dryness.

CERCIDIPHYLLUM japonicum

clusters of bell-shaped blue-violet blossoms.

Culture. Bellflowers prefer good garden soil, well-drained and reasonably fertile. All will take regular watering, though the Balkan species (especially Serbian bellflower) are somewhat drought-tolerant in shade.

Good companions. *Bergenia, Corydalis, ferns, Hemerocallis, Hosta, Lilium, Thalictrum.*

🌾
CERCIDIPHYLLUM japonicum

Katsura tree
Deciduous tree
Hardy to –30°F/–34°C
Part shade/regular water

Katsura tree has year-round visual appeal. In early spring, a haze of tiny, reddish purple flowers covers the bare branches. Soon young bronzy foliage emerges, maturing to redbudlike blue-green leaves 2 to 4 inches long. Throughout spring and summer, the leaves show red tints, and then in autumn they change to brilliant yellow or red.

Katsura tree is an elegant choice wherever sunlight is dappled or restricted for half the day. Young specimens grow at a moderate rate, but the pace slows as they become established. Eventually you can expect a tree to 50 feet high and wide—always open enough to filter breezes and light. Trained to a single trunk, the canopy will remain narrow and upright for many years. If you encourage several trunks, you'll achieve a broadly spreading tree with branches angling out and up, carrying foliage in horizontal tiers.

Culture. Healthy growth occurs in a good, deep, neutral to slightly acid soil. Water regularly during dry periods.

Good companions. *Camellia, Hydrangea, Ilex, Kalmia, Osmanthus, Rhododendron, Viburnum.*

🌾
CERCIS canadensis

Eastern redbud
Deciduous tree
Hardy to –20°F/–29°C
Part shade/moderate water

Redbuds are part of the annual fanfare announcing the arrival of spring. Small purplish pink blossoms literally cover twigs, branches, main limbs, even trunks. Then flattened, beanlike seedpods form as the trees leaf out, much in evidence as red-brown pendants after the leaves fall in autumn.

CERCIS canadensis

Leaves can reach 6 inches long, each broadly rounded with heart-shaped base and pointed tip. Bluish green in spring and summer, they change to bright yellow in autumn. Trees grow fairly rapidly, forming a somewhat irregular canopy 25 to 35 feet high; older trees tend to carry branches in horizontal tiers.

Named selections offer blossoms in white, wine red, or pink. 'Flame' has the standard blue-toned pink blossoms, but they are double and rosebudlike. Rich purple foliage is the hallmark of 'Forest Pansy'.

Culture. Eastern redbud is easy to grow in average, well-drained soil. Water regularly for several years to get it established; after that, moderate watering is sufficient. Locate this tree in light shade or dappled sunlight from taller trees.

Good companions. *Convallaria, Dicentra, Helleborus, Rhododendron (particularly azaleas), Viola.*

🌾
CIMICIFUGA

Bugbane
Deciduous perennials
Hardy to –35°F/–37°C
Part shade/regular water

Although bugbanes have sizeable foliage clumps and tall flowering stems, their delicacy of detail relieves any sense of massiveness. Mounds of coarsely fernlike leaves may grow 2½ feet high, with slender, branched stems rising above them to end in elongated "foxtails" of small, bristly white flowers.

Black snakeroot, *C. racemosa,* produces upright blossom spikes on 6-foot stems in midsummer. In contrast, the Kamchatka bugbane, *C. simplex,* bears arching floral plumes on 4-foot stems in autumn. A striking autumn-flowering accent is provided by *C. ramosa* 'Atropurpurea', which can raise its clustered flowers on 7-foot stems above purplish foliage.

Culture. The dappled, filtered, or partial shade of woodland margins suits the bugbanes. Plant them in good soil, liberally enriched with organic matter, and water regularly.

CIMICIFUGA racemosa

Good companions. *Anemone, Hosta, Filipendula, Ligularia, Thalictrum, Trollius.*

❧ CLEMATIS

Clematis
Deciduous and evergreen vines
Hardy to –20°F/–29°C except as noted
Part shade/regular water

Diversity is the keynote of this genus, which includes some of the most popular flowering vines. Some species and hybrids make modest-sized vines to 8 feet or so—positively shrimpy compared to such gargantuan tree-eaters as *C. armandii* and *C. montana*. Flowers may be small and delicate—like the bell-shaped blooms of *C. texensis*—or flat and saucer-size, as in many hybrids. Plants may blossom in spring, summer, spring and summer, or autumn—even late winter in mild-winter climates. Small-flowered species run to pastels and white, but you'll find vibrant blue, lavender, violet, purple, pink, and red among the large-flowered hybrids.

The true flowers are tiny; what appear to be flower petals are really petal-like sepals surrounding the flower clusters. After flowering, many plants produce decorative, silky seed tassels. Vines climb by coiling their leafstalks around branches, string, or wire.

Standard advice is to plant clematis where its roots will be shaded and cool but where stems can climb into sunlight.

CLEMATIS montana 'Rubens'

CLETHRA alnifolia

It is also true that most will thrive in partial shade, filtered sunlight, even high shade where there is plenty of light—especially in warmer climates where sunlight is more intense.

Mail-order specialists offer the best selection. If a local nursery stocks any clematis, they are likely to be flashy, large-flowered hybrids. All these are lovely garden subjects; choose according to color preference.

Among other worthy types is *C. montana*, the anemone clematis, which is hardy to –10°F/–23°C. Its rampant vines offer a massive early spring show of flowers resembling those of Japanese anemone (see *Anemone*, page 63). White aging to pink is the usual color, but selections 'Rubens' and 'Tetrarose' are deep pink. Another rapid grower, to about 20 feet, is the evergreen clematis, *C. armandii*, hardy to 0°F/–18°C. Its glossy, tapered leaflets form a handsome backdrop for a froth of fragrant white blossoms in early spring. Golden clematis, *C. tangutica*, is more restrained, growing to about 15 feet with finely divided foliage. Through summer and into autumn, it produces 2- to 4-inch yellow flowers shaped like hanging lanterns.

Culture. All clematis prefer good, fast-draining soil amply fortified with organic matter. A regular moisture supply is especially important during active growth. Mulch plants to conserve moisture and keep soil cool.

Good companions. *Aconitum, Alchemilla, Aruncus, Astilbe, Cimicifuga, Filipendula, Thalictrum.*

❧ CLETHRA alnifolia

Summersweet, sweet pepperbush
Deciduous shrub
Hardy to –40°F/–40°C
Part shade/regular water

The common name summersweet covers both the season and the pleasing, spicy fragrance of this shrub's blossoms. Growing upright to about 10 feet, the plant expands gradually as new stems grow from the ground. Thin-textured, 4-inch oval leaves are dark green until autumn conditions turn them bright yellow or orange. For a month or more in midsummer, 4- to 6-inch foxtail-like spikes of small white flowers appear at branch ends; for color, look for pale pink 'Rosea' and darker pink 'Pinkspire'.

Culture.
Summersweet thrives under the same conditions as rhododendrons—organically enriched, well-drained, neutral to acid soil—but also will grow well in perpetually damp soil alongside a pond or stream.

CLIVIA miniata

Good companions. *Alchemilla, Filipendula, Rhododendron, Thalictrum, Tiarella, Trollius.*

❧ CLIVIA miniata

Clivia, Kaffir lily
Evergreen perennial
Hardy to 25°F/–4°C
Part to full shade/regular water

Fortunate gardeners in mild-winter regions can grow clivia in the ground, where it will form truly impressive clumps or drifts of leathery, strap-shaped leaves. Each leaf grows to 1½ feet long, a single plant forming a virtual fountain of foliage. In midwinter to early spring, thick 2-foot stems are crowned by a great cluster of funnel-shaped, 2-inch blossoms—typically orange with yellow throat, but ranging from pale yellow to nearly red in hybrid strains. 'Flame' is a superior selection in hot red-orange.

After flowers finish, you may be treated to a cluster of showy orange or red berries.

Culture. In frost-free and nearly frostless regions, plant clivia in the ground in good, organically enriched soil. Water regularly from winter through summer, cut back to moderate watering in autumn—but never let the leaves wilt. Plantings can exist for years before they have to be divided.

Where winter temperatures drop below clivia's tolerance, you can grow plants in pots or tubs and move them in winter to frost-free shelter (even a cool room in the house). Use a deep container (at least 12 inches) just a bit wider than the root mass: clivia flowers well when rootbound. For best bloom, give container plants liquid fertilizer monthly in spring and summer.

Good companions. *Ajuga, Aucuba, ferns, Heucherella, Polygonatum, Soleirolia, Tiarella.*

❧

CONVALLARIA *majalis*

Lily-of-the-valley
Deciduous perennial
Hardy to –40°F/–40°C
Part shade/regular water

Simple elegance and delicious scent have endeared lily-of-the-valley to generations

CONVALLARIA majalis

of gardeners. From each rhizome (called a "pip") come 2 or 3 broad, lance-shaped leaves to 9 inches long and, in early spring, 12 to 20 waxy white bells hanging from a slender stem. Bulb specialists sometimes offer forms with pale pink or double white blossoms.

In time, plants spread into a solid carpet, making an attractive ground cover beneath deciduous trees and shrubs or large clumps among other perennials that share their need for light shade or filtered sunlight.

Culture. Lily-of-the-valley thrives only where winter temperatures reliably dip below freezing (32°F/0°C). Plant pips in good soil amended with a generous helping of organic matter. Set out in clumps or drifts, 1 to 2 inches deep and 4 to 6 inches apart. Water regularly, even when dormant and leafless. Before new growth emerges each year, top dress with compost, leaf mold, or ground bark to maintain the organic content of the soil.

Good companions. *Camellia, Dicentra, Enkianthus, Pieris, Primula, Rhododendron, Tiarella.*

❧

CORNUS

Dogwood
Deciduous trees, shrubs, perennial
Hardiness varies
Part shade/regular water

The popular tree-size dogwoods grow naturally at forest margins where high shade from larger trees moderates sunlight. Most shrubby types of dogwood accept some shade but don't demand it. The one ground cover species, though, is for shady locations only.

The most popular tree-sized dogwood, without question, is flowering dogwood, *C. florida,* native to eastern North America. Trees are hardy to –20°F/–29°C. In spring they provide a massive floral display in white or pink before leaves emerge; in autumn, flame-colored foliage takes center stage. Growth is pyramidal to flat-topped, the

branches extending out in tiers. In the Northwest and parts of Northern California, the Pacific dogwood, *C. nuttallii,* gives a good spring show of large white blossoms (after leaf-out) on a relatively narrow tree to 50 feet tall. Trees flower again, less profusely, in late summer. Pacific dogwoods are hardy to 0°F/–18°C.

Unfortunately, both flowering and Pacific dogwood species are pest- and disease-prone in their native territories, where their planting is something of a risk.

CORNUS canadensis

Hybrids of flowering dogwood and Japanese dogwood *(C. kousa)*— now designated *C. × rutgersensis*— take after the flowering dogwood in hardiness and appearance (though blossoms appear with the leaves in late spring). Most importantly, they resist the debilitating anthracnose fungus. Trees make broad pyramids to 20 feet or more. White- and pink-flowered selections are available.

Shrubby dogwoods usually lack the conspicuous flowers of the tree types, but they compensate with colorful stems and, in some selections, variegated foliage. Small, creamy white to greenish white flowers cluster among the leaves; small fruits (usually white) follow by late summer or early autumn, ripening before foliage turns bright red. All will grow in light or filtered shade; variegated foliage forms need some shade to prevent leaf burn.

Tatarian dogwood, *C. alba,* is hardy to –50°F/–46°C. Blood red stems form an upright-spreading thicket to 10 feet high. 'Argenteomarginata' ('Elegantissima') features white-edged, grayish green leaves. Bloodtwig dogwood, *C. sanguinea,* is hardy to –30°F/–34°C. It's a bit

CORYDALIS lutea

taller and more upright than Tatarian dogwood, with black fruits and darker red stems.

Redtwig or red-osier dogwood, *C. stolonifera* (often sold as *C. sericea*), is hardy to –50°F/–46°C. The basic species grows vigorously into a thicket 15 feet high, expanding by underground stems and tip-rooting branches. The selection 'Flaviramea' has showy yellow stems; 'Silver and Gold' has variegated leaves. Shorter variants include the Colorado redtwig (*C. s. coloradensis*), to 6 feet; *C. s. baileyi*, 6 to 8 feet; and *C. s.* 'Kelseyi' ('Nana'), about 1½ feet.

Bunchberry, *C. canadensis,* is a woodland carpet plant, hardy to –40°F/–40°C. Its 1- to 2-inch leaves make an even cover to 6 inches high, decorated in spring by small, white-bracted flowers and in late summer by edible red fruits. Leaves turn yellow as weather chills, then the entire plant dies to the ground.

Culture. Tree dogwoods prefer a slightly acid, well-drained soil with water during dry periods. Shrubby species will really prosper in soil that is damp, such as beside a pond, though ordinary garden watering is sufficient. Ground-covering bunchberry needs a forest-floor soil: somewhat acid, moist but well-drained, with plenty of organic matter. Small starts may not establish; for best success,

COTULA squalida

transplant clumps with a piece of rotten log attached.

Good companions. *Ferns, Kalmia, Mahonia, Rhododendron, Viburnum.*

❧ *CORYDALIS lutea*

Corydalis
Deciduous perennial
Hardy to –10°F/–23°C
Part shade/regular water

Low clumps of fernlike, gray-green leaves call out the corydalis plant's close relationship to bleeding-heart *(Dicentra).* The flowers, though, are distinctly different: small clusters of down-hanging, nearly tubular ¾-inch-long yellow blossoms dot the foliage for a lengthy summer blooming period.

Its 12- to 15-inch height makes this a fine foreground plant in locations where soil is always moist and high-branching trees cast light or filtered shade.

Culture. Good, organically enriched soil that is steadily moist (but not soggy) ensures success with corydalis. Under these conditions, volunteer seedlings will enlarge the planting.

Good companions. *Aquilegia, Campanula, Dicentra, ferns, Leucothoe, Lilium, Primula.*

❧ *COTULA squalida*

New Zealand brass buttons
Deciduous to evergreen perennial
ground cover
Hardy to –10°F/–23°C
Part shade/regular water

Here's a ground-hugging mat of a plant to use as a modest-scale ground cover or even to plant between paving stones. Bronzy green, hairy, fernlike leaves spread out flat on the ground, making a solid backdrop for ¼-inch, buttonlike yellow flowers during summer. Cover is solid but not impenetrable: you can plant it over spring bulbs, and it will hide

CYCLAMEN coum

their traces after the bulb flowers and foliage die down.

Culture. Plants need moist soil, organically amended but not especially rich. Where winter temperatures remain above 10°F/–12°C, plants are evergreen.

Good companions. *Aspidistra, Bergenia, Euonymus, Lilium, Liriope, Trillium.*

❧ *CYCLAMEN*

Cyclamen
Deciduous tuberous perennials
Hardy to 0°F/–18°C
Part to full shade/moderate water

The showy, large-flowered but frost-tender florists' cyclamen (*C. persicum*) is a familiar potted plant for wintertime gift-giving. Less well known are numerous other cyclamen species suited to growing outdoors—smaller, less showy, but utterly charming. Collectively, they are referred to as the "hardy cyclamen." They make handsome drifts or a small-scale ground cover under trees or large shrubs, or along paths where you can appreciate the intricate leaf patterning.

Although the hardy cyclamen species are smaller than the typical *C. persicum* gift plant, they are built along the same lines. Flowers consist of elongated, twisted petals flaring back from a central ring; they come individually on stems that rise above the leaves or above bare ground before leaves emerge. Colors range from white, lilac, and pink to rosy red; often the ring from which petals depart is a

(Continued on page 79)

ENCYCLOPEDIA OF SHADE PLANTS

77

CAREX • Sedge

Hardy to –20°F/–29°C except as noted.
Although sedges are not true grasses, their appearance puts them easily into that company. The following species offer foliage that departs from basic green.

Leather leaf sedge, *C. buchananii*, is hardy to –10°F/–23°C. Reedlike, curly-tipped leaves in a striking rusty bronze color are upright but arching to 2 to 3 feet tall. Bowles' golden sedge, *C. elata* 'Bowles' Golden', makes fountainlike clumps 2 feet tall, the leaves brilliant yellow from spring well into summer, then green the rest of the year.

Blue sedge, *C. flacca (C. glauca)*, grows as a slowly spreading ground cover, making a 6- to 12-inch-high grassy turf of blue-gray. You can plant it where it gets light foot traffic—even clipping it like a lawn. Variegated Japanese sedge, *C. morrowii expallida (C. m.* 'Variegata'), forms shaggy, foot-tall mounds of arching white leaves with green margins. In *C. e.* 'Aurea-variegata' (*C. m.* 'Goldband'), the variegation is in yellow.

Sedges are happy in partial or light shade in all climates. Give them regular watering, even poorly drained soil: they thrive in boggy soil at the margins of ponds and streams.

HAKONECHLOA macra 'Aureola' • Japanese forest grass

Hardy to –30°F/–34°C. You might mistake this grass for a very small bamboo. Its clumps of slender, leaning to arching 1½-foot-long stems bear lax, yellow-striped leaves that clasp the stems in bamboo fashion. A single clump makes a low hummock of lush foliage; a drift planting becomes a sea of leaves about a foot high. *H. m.* 'Albo-variegata' has leaves edged in white.

As befits a forest native, this grass prefers partial shade and soil that's a bit acid, well drained, and enriched with organic matter. It grows best where sum-

ORNAMENTAL GRASSES

❧

Grasses may seem more naturally paired in the imagination with sunshine than with shade. But the four grasses and one grasslike sedge described here find a congenial home in shade.

mer is cool to moderate. Water regularly for best performance and appearance.

MILIUM effusum 'Aureum' • Bowles' golden grass

Hardy to –10°F/–23°C. This grass is yellow all over, from the greenish gold foliage to the yellow stems and flowers. Clumps of upright-arching leaves reach 1½ to 2 feet high, the slender stems and loose flower heads extending well above.

As a native of moist woodlands, Bowles' golden grass will thrive in garden settings that are similar. Give it light shade or dappled sunlight and organically enriched soil. Regular watering keeps it looking good.

MISCANTHUS sinensis • Eulalia grass

Hardy to –20°F/–29°C. Here is a dual-purpose landscape grass, at home in both light shade and sun. Eulalia grass and its named selections are robust growers,

HAKONECHLOA macra 'Aureola'

PENNISETUM alopecuroides

most of them making tall clumps suitable for accents and background planting. Foliage usually reaches 5 to 6 feet high, flowering stems adding another 1 to 3 feet in summer and autumn. Foliage turns golden tan in late autumn.

Maiden grass, *M. s.* 'Gracillimus', has particularly narrow, silvery green arching leaves and beige flower clusters that are loose and feathery. In the selections 'Variegatus' and 'Silberpfeil' ('Silver Arrow'), leaves are broader and have lengthwise white stripes. 'Morning Light' has distinctly white-margined, silvery green leaves; 'Zebrinus' features lateral striping in yellow and green. 'Yaku Jima' ('Yakushima') grows about 3 feet high, making feathery clumps that turn red in autumn.

All eulalia grasses grow into dense clumps but are noninvasive. Plant them in well-drained, fairly good soil; for best appearance, water regularly.

PENNISETUM • Fountain grass

Hardiness varies. The name "fountain grass" is totally descriptive: clumps are fine-textured sprays of arching foliage. At flowering time, foxtail-like floral plumes rise above the clumps.

Chinese pennisetum, *P. alopecuroides*, is hardy to –20°F/–29°C. Clumps of dark green leaves grow about 3 to 4 feet high and wide, with pinkish tan flower plumes floating above the clumps from late summer into autumn. The selection 'Moudry' has striking black flower plumes; 'Hameln' has white plumes over foliage that grows just 2 to 3 feet high.

Oriental fountain grass, *P. orientale*, is hardy to 0°F/–18°C. Its light green leaves grow 1½ to 2 feet high, complemented by pinkish plumes rising a foot higher.

Plant both fountain grasses in lightly shaded locations where soil is reasonably good. Water during dry periods.

darker or contrasting color. Fleshy heart-shaped or rounded leaves are carried on thick stalks 4 to 6 inches above the ground. In most species, leaves are marbled or veined in lovely patterns of silvery white or light green.

Each foliage clump springs from a tuber that gets bigger each year. Tubers do not produce increases, but new plants often pop up as volunteer seedlings.

Time of flowering varies. Among the more common species, *C. repandum* blooms in spring, *C. hederifolium* and *C. purpurascens* in summer, *C. cilicium* in autumn on into winter, and both *C. atkinsii* and *C. coum* in winter.

Culture. Hardy cyclamen are woodland-wildflower plants suited to light shade or sunlight filtered through foliage.

Give tubers well-drained soil liberally amended with organic matter. Water regularly during dry periods while plants are in leaf. All but *C. purpurascens* go through a dormant, leafless period after flowering, during which time they need only occasional watering until growth resumes.

Good companions. *Camellia, Enkianthus, Kalmia, Polygonatum, Rhododendron, Trillium.*

❧

CYMBALARIA muralis

Kenilworth ivy
Evergreen perennial
Hardy to −20°F/−29°C
Part to full shade/regular water

Its dainty, diminutive charm masks Kenilworth ivy's rugged constitution. Stems creep along the ground, bearing lobed, ivylike leaves no larger than an

CYMBALARIA muralis

DAPHNE × burkwoodii 'Carol Mackie'

inch across. Little snapdragonlike lavender flowers dot the foliage carpet in spring and summer; with some searching, you may find a white-flowered form labeled 'Alba' or 'Nana Alba'.

Stems root at joints where they contact moist soil, and volunteer seedlings are common. To some gardeners, this makes Kenilworth ivy almost a weed. But it is a sure and attractive success as a ground cover or patch plant in moist shade, and unwanted plants are easily removed.

Culture. Nothing could be simpler: Kenilworth ivy needs only average soil and regular watering. Plants are attractive spilling from pots and hanging baskets; they'll even grow in chinks of stone walls.

Good companions. *Asarum, Aspidistra, Clivia, Convallaria, ferns, Liriope, Polygonatum.*

❧

DAPHNE

Daphne
Deciduous and evergreen shrubs
Hardiness varies
Part shade/moderate water

The daphnes are enjoyed for their flowers in winter or spring, but they are positively cherished for their fragrance. Only one species lacks a sweet perfume. Plants have a reputation for being temperamental—not always easy to establish, sometimes short-lived. But many gardeners consider the risks well worth taking.

The deciduous February daphne, *D. mezereum*, is hardy to −30°F/−34°C. Rosy purple flowers appear along its upright branches in late winter or early spring,

followed by red berries. The selection 'Alba' has white flowers and yellow fruits. Plants are rather stiff and angular, to 4 feet high, with oval 3-inch leaves.

In the coldest regions, *D. × burkwoodii* (also hardy to −30°F/−34°C) loses its leaves in winter, but in warmer-winter regions it is evergreen. This compact, rather rounded plant grows to 4 feet, its narrow leaves nearly obscured by late spring flowers. The standard color is white fading to pink; 'Somerset' is pink from start to finish. 'Carol Mackie' has light pink flowers and a yellow band around each leaf.

Deciduous lilac daphne, *D. genkwa*, is hardy to −10°F/−23°C. Its complete lack of fragrance is compensated for by its floral profusion, transforming each bare branch into a wand of delicate lilac in midspring; white fruits follow the flowers. Growth is gracefully rounded, 3 to 4 feet high and wide.

Intoxicatingly sweet winter daphne, *D. odora*, is evergreen and hardy to 5°F/−15°C. This is the prima donna of the genus, needing just the right conditions for success: perfect drainage in an organically amended soil, and just enough water to keep from wilting. At its best, it is a rounded-spreading plant to 4 feet high (sometimes twice that), with leathery dark green oval leaves. Flowers cluster at branch ends in late winter, typically pink-throated white but entirely white in one form. Commonly-grown 'Marginata' has pink flowers and yellow-edged leaves.

Note: all daphne parts, especially the fruits, are poisonous to ingest.

Culture. Daphnes need organically enriched, well-drained soil, cool and moist but never waterlogged. Prepare soil well, water judiciously, and mulch beneath the plant.

Good companions. *Epimedium, Fothergilla, Gaultheria, Leucothoe, Rhododendron.*

DICENTRA

Bleeding heart
Deciduous perennials
Hardy to –35°F/–37°C
Part shade/regular water

Distinctive heart-shaped flowers— usually in pink rather than red—give bleeding hearts their common name. Flowers appear suspended above almost feathery foliage, a picture of elegant delicacy.

Common bleeding heart, *Digitalis spectabilis,* is the largest, with branched stems to 3 feet high carrying nearly horizontal sprays of pink-and-white blossoms. 'Pantaloons' and 'Alba' are selections with all-white flowers. Plants begin to die down after late spring flowering and are dormant by midsummer.

Fringed bleeding heart, *D. eximia,* and western bleeding heart, *D. formosa,* are similar low, spreading clumps of fluffy foliage, above which bare stems hold clusters of hearts. Fringed bleeding heart's blue-gray foliage grows 1½ feet high; western bleeding heart produces foot-high blue-green leaves. White-flowered selections of both are available.

Probable hybrids of the latter two species include rosy red 'Bountiful', cherry pink 'Luxuriant' (the best choice for mild winter/hot summer regions), and carmine red 'Adrian Bloom'.

Culture. Plant all bleeding hearts in woodland conditions: well-drained, organically enriched soil where roots can be cool and moist but not soggy.

Good companions. *Bergenia, Convallaria, Digitalis, Epimedium, ferns, Hosta, Mertensia, Trillium.*

DIGITALIS purpurea

DICENTRA spectabilis

DIGITALIS

Foxglove
Evergreen biennial and perennials
Hardiness varies
Part shade/regular water

The classic foxglove is biennial *D. purpurea,* hardy to –20°F/–29°C. From clumps of large, furry, tongue-shaped leaves rise 6-foot stems bearing pendent, thimble-shaped flowers in white, lavender, pink, or purple. Plants flower the second year after germination; volunteer seedlings are common, so after that you usually have a crop ready to bloom each spring.

Perennial foxgloves are similar but shorter, with flower stems around 3 feet tall. *Digitalis* × *mertonensis,* hardy to –20°F/–29°C, features coppery pink flowers; despite being a hybrid, it comes true from seed. Yellow foxglove, *D. grandiflora* (also sold as *D. ambigua*), is hardy to –30°F/–34°C. Flowers are pale yellow, lightly spotted brown inside.

Culture. Give foxgloves filtered sunlight, partial shade, or light shade. Soil should be good and well-drained, kept moist in dry periods.

Good companions. *Alchemilla, Campanula, Dicentra, ferns, Hemerocallis, Hosta, Thalictrum.*

DORONICUM

Leopard's bane
Deciduous perennials
Hardy to –30°F/–34°C
Part shade/regular water

The leopard's banes come on with great gusto in spring, producing mounds of heart-shaped leaves and upright stems of showy yellow daisy flowers. Then they pull a disappearing act, dying down completely by the middle of summer.

Plantain leopard's bane, *D. plantagineum,* is the larger of the two commonly-sold species. Flowering stems grow 2½ to 3 feet high, bearing 2- to 4-inch daisies. Shorter *D. cordatum* also circulates as *D. caucasicum, D. columnae,* and *D. orientale.* Typical flower stems grow 1½ feet high, each bearing a single 2-inch flower; 'Finesse' and 'Magnificum' are taller and larger-blossomed.

DORONICUM cordatum

Culture. Good, organically enriched soil and woodland-edge conditions will sustain leopard's banes. Keep soil moist while plants are in leaf; after they've died down, moderate watering will suffice. Performance flags after several years; divide clumps in early spring to rejuvenate plants.

Good companions. *Brunnera, ferns, Helleborus, Hosta, Mertensia, Myosotis.*

DUCHESNEA indica

Indian mock strawberry
Evergreen perennial ground cover
Hardy to –30°F/–34°C
Part to full shade/moderate water

You could easily mistake this plant for a strawberry. The foliage looks like strawberry, and plants spread in strawberry

DUCHESNEA indica

fashion by runners, rooting as they spread. The ½-inch red fruits complete the picture—until you taste them. Flavor (or lack of it) aside, there are two other telltale differences. Flowers of Indian mock strawberry are yellow, not white; and both its flowers and fruits are carried above the foliage, whereas true strawberries nestle among or beneath the leaves.

In shade, the foliage rises to about 6 inches. Growth is rapid, sometimes even invasive, but it's easy to curb or control the spread.

Culture. Indian mock strawberry flourishes in just average soil with moderate watering. Under "good" conditions—rich soil, regular watering—it becomes too successful.

Good companions. *Arbutus, Aucuba, Berberis, Euonymus, Mahonia, Nandina, Rhamnus, Ribes.*

❧ ENKIANTHUS

Enkianthus
Deciduous shrubs
Hardiness varies
Part shade/regular water

Their rhododendron cousins have more flash, but these shrubs possess a

ENKIANTHUS campanulatus

beauty of detail that grows on you. After pointed oval leaves form in early spring, countless little bell-shaped blossoms hang in clusters beneath groups of leaves at branch ends. Plants grow upright, but branching typically is in horizontal tiers. The orange or red autumn foliage is spectacular.

Redvein enkianthus, *E. campanulatus,* is the hardiest species, tolerating temperatures down to –20°F/–29°C. The plant in time may grow 20 feet tall; its ½-inch greenish yellow bell-flowers are veined in red. *E. c. palibinii* has dark red veins on a lighter red flower, 'Albiflorus' has totally white blossoms, and 3-foot-high 'Red Bells' has red flowers.

Two species are hardy to –10°F/–23°C. White bells adorn *E. cernuus,* a bushy plant about 10 feet high, but more frequently available is its red-flowered form *E. c. rubens* (*E. c.* 'Matsudai'). Shorter (around 8 feet) *E. perulatus* is noteworthy for its profusion of smaller white bells before spring leaf-out.

Culture. Like most members of the heath family, *Enkianthus* species need slightly acid soil that is very well drained but can hold moisture. Liberally amend soil with organic matter (peat moss and ground bark are good), plant so that the top of the root ball sits higher than the level of the surrounding soil, and mulch well. Always water during dry periods.

Good companions. *Alchemilla, Camellia, Epimedium, ferns, Franklinia, Gaultheria, Rhododendron.*

❧ EPIMEDIUM

Epimedium, barrenwort, bishop's hat
Deciduous and evergreen perennials
Hardy to –30°F/–34°C
Part to full shade/regular water

You would hardly guess that these neat and elegant ground cover plants are related to the spiny barberries and prickly mahonias. In the epimediums, delicacy and charm replace formidable defense.

EPIMEDIUM × youngianum 'Niveum'

Growing from a dense network of underground stems, wiry leafstalks support heart-shaped leaflets that overlap to form foliage clumps. New growth is a show in itself when it emerges bronzy pink. Leaves become green by summer but change again to reddish bronze in autumn. In spring, wiry flower stems hold airy blossom sprays above the foliage—just above or well above, depending on the species. Flower shape varies from cup-and-saucer to saucer alone; some species have columbinelike spurs.

Among deciduous species and hybrids, *E. grandiflorum* claims the largest blossoms—2 inches. They are red and violet with white spur, but named selections offer white, pink, lavender, and red flowers. Foliage grows to about 12 inches high. The hybrid *E. × youngianum* makes 8-inch-high clumps of pale green leaves; named selections have white or pink flowers.

Evergreen epimediums offer, besides persistent foliage, a different floral color range. Persian epimedium, *E. pinnatum,* makes foot-high clumps of glossy leaflets that set off yellow blossoms. Foot-tall *E. × rubrum* produces sprays of flowers in red with yellow or white; specialists also sell pink- and white-flowered selections.

Culture. Epimediums appreciate a slightly acid soil well amended with organic matter. For best appearance, shear off the foliage in late winter or early spring, just before new growth emerges.

Good companions. *Bergenia, Camellia, Dicentra, ferns, Helleborus, Rhododendron.*

EUONYMUS fortunei 'Gracilis'

🌿
EUONYMUS fortunei

Euonymus
Evergreen shrub and vine
Hardy to –20°F/–29°C
Part shade/moderate water

Wherever you live, this is a fine evergreen, with attractive form and lustrous, leathery oval leaves. It's one of the few broad-leafed evergreens to survive in truly cold-winter regions. But this plant is a changeling, so it pays to know the exact name of the form or selection you are buying. Immature growth is vining—sprawling on the ground or attaching by aerial rootlets to any vertical surface it encounters. In time, a mature vining plant bears flowers; cuttings taken from these stems produce shrubby plants.

Many selections have been named and marketed. *Euonymus radicans,* once thought to be the basic wild species, was later determined to be a naturally-occurring variety of *E. fortunei.* Even so, some nurseries still sell named clones as forms of "*E. radicans.*" Whenever you see a label that says "*E. radicans* 'So-and-So'," translate "*radicans*" to "*fortunei*"—except when you see *E. fortunei radicans*: this is the correct name for the common winter creeper (see the following).

Plants labeled *E. fortunei* with no other qualification should be sprawling semishrubs whose branches will root where they touch soil or climb whenever they can attach to a support. Leaves are dark green, to 2½ inches long. More widely available are various truly shrubby selections in a variety of sizes, growth habits, and foliage colors. All have scalloped leaves 1 to 2 inches long. Flowers are insignificant; a few produce showy orange fruits in autumn. Many variegated-leaf selections also are available.

Common winter creeper, *E. f. radicans,* is a trailing or vining plant with inch-long, dark green leaves. The purple-leaf winter creeper is *E. f.* 'Colorata'. Its growth habit is the same as for common winter creeper, though this plant makes a more even carpet as a ground cover. Leaves turn dark purple in cold weather.

Culture. This comes close to being a "plant it and forget it" item. There are no soil preferences, and established plants need only moderate watering during dry periods.

Good companions. *Aegopodium, Berberis, Duchesnea, Hedera, Juniperus, Mahonia, Myrtus, Taxus.*

🌿
× FATSHEDERA lizei

Fatshedera
Evergreen vining shrub
Hardy to 5°F/–15°C
Part to full shade/regular water

To visualize this plant, imagine roughly equal parts of its parents—Japanese aralia (*Fatsia japonica*) and English ivy (*Hedera helix*). The 6- to 8-inch lobed leaves and their thick stems are aralia-like. But the stems are lax and trailing, suggesting the ivy part of the equation—though they don't attach to surfaces as ivy does. The usual plant has highly polished green leaves, but the form 'Variegata' features leaves with white margins.

× FATSHEDERA lizei

Use fatshedera as a bold-textured ground cover, cutting back or pegging down any stems that attempt to grow upright. Or train it as a free-form sculptural espalier on a trellis or wall, making sure to provide a way to tie the stems in place. Stems tend to grow unbranched in a straight line. To encourage branching, pinch tip growth or cut stems back to where you want branches to form.

Culture. True to its ancestry, this is a notably unfussy plant. It will grow in virtually any soil. For best growth, it needs regular moisture but not a saturated soil.

Good companions. *Acanthus, Aspidistra, Aucuba, Clivia, Hypericum, Juniperus.*

🌿
FATSIA japonica

Japanese aralia
Evergreen shrub
Hardy to 5°F/–15°C
Part to full shade/regular water

Bold, tropical, architectural—these words all describe Japanese aralia. Its leaves are shaped like deeply lobed fans, up to 16 inches across with a surface like dark green lacquer. The long leafstalks spring directly from a canelike stem that rises 5 to 8 feet from the ground with little or no branching. Plants are upright and narrow at first, becoming broader and more rounded as more stems grow.

Large, branched flower sprays carry ball-shaped clusters of tiny white blossoms; these are followed by small, black, berrylike fruits. The selection 'Variegata' has cream or yellow leaf margins and is slightly less vigorous; 'Moseri' is naturally low-growing.

FATSIA japonica

FILIPENDULA purpurea

Culture. You can grow Japanese aralia in a broad range of soils, from poorly- to well-drained, as long as you make sure the soil doesn't stay saturated.

The plant can be shaped various ways. You can emphasize the naturally vertical, leggy look by selectively removing new stems as they sprout from the base. Or you can encourage a bushier plant by cutting back stems to any height, forcing branches to grow from beneath the cuts.

Good companions. *Aspidistra, Bergenia, Buxus, Clivia, Hedera, Juniperus, Trachelospermum.*

❧

FILIPENDULA

Meadowsweet
Deciduous perennials
Hardiness varies
Part shade/regular water

For garden effect, think of the meadowsweet as a larger *Astilbe* (see page 65). Dense plumes of tiny flowers float over clumps of good-looking, jagged-edged leaves.

Tallest of the commonly available species is 6- to 8-foot *F. rubra*, known as queen of the prairie. As befits a prairie native, it is hardy: to −40°F/−40°C. Bright pink is the usual flower color, but the selected form 'Venusta' has darker, purplish pink flowers on 4- to 6-foot stems.

European queen of the meadow, *F. ulmaria*, is equally hardy, raising creamy white flowers to 6 feet. Selections with decorative foliage are more widely grown than the basic species. Leaves of 'Variegata' are margined in light yellow; 'Aurea' has bright yellow leaves but inconsequential flowers.

Japanese meadowsweet, *F. purpurea*, takes temperatures only to −10°F/−23°C. From clumps of maplelike leaves rise reddish 4-foot stems carrying plumes of deep cherry pink flowers. Its form 'Alba' is white-flowered, while 'Elegans' offers white blossoms with red stamens.

Culture. The meadowsweets need a good, organically enriched soil and regular watering (at a minimum) during dry periods. They are good pondside plants, reveling in always-moist soil.

Good companions. *Astilbe, Carex (see "Ornamental Grasses," page 78), Hosta, Ligularia.*

❧

FOTHERGILLA

Fothergilla
Deciduous shrubs
Hardy to −10°F/−23°C
Part to full shade/regular water

The various fothergillas possess a subtle beauty. Their early spring flowering is pretty but not flashy, and their autumn foliage display is colorful but hardly blinding.

White flowers appear at branch tips before, or just as, leaves emerge. They consist entirely of stamens, resembling small bottlebrushes. Oval leaves give you yellow, orange, and purplish red shades as their autumn finale.

Dwarf fothergilla, *F. gardenii*, reaches about 3 feet high with a spreading habit. Its selection 'Mt. Airy' is a bit larger in all parts, and its bluish green leaves offer especially good autumn color. Considerably taller, to 9 feet, is *F. major* (including plants formerly known as *F. monticola*)—upright-growing, taller than broad.

Culture. Give fothergillas a fairly good, slightly acid soil amended with organic matter. For the best autumn foliage color, locate plants in dappled sunlight or in high shade where there's plenty of light. If you need to shape plants, prune in spring right after flowering.

FOTHERGILLA gardenii

Good companions. *Alchemilla, Aquilegia, Dicentra, Helleborus, Hosta, Rhododendron.*

❧

FRANCOA ramosa

Bridal wreath, maiden's wreath
Evergreen perennial
Hardy to 5°F/−15°C
Part shade/regular water

Here is a charming, summer-flowering perennial for massing in the foreground of woodland-style gardens. Like its relatives × *Heucherella* (page 87) and *Tiarella* (page 106), it produces attractive foliage clumps, each large leaf lobed with wavy edges. From these low mounds rise wiry stems 2 to 3 feet high bearing spikes of small white (sometimes pink), long-lasting flowers.

Culture. Average, well-drained soil amended with organic matter satisfies bridal wreath. Best flowering occurs in part shade, dappled sunlight, or high shade with plenty of light.

Good companions. *Camellia, Digitalis, Hosta, Liriope, Platycodon, Primula, Rhododendron.*

FRANCOA ramosa

FRANKLINIA alatamaha

❧

FRANKLINIA alatamaha

Franklinia
Deciduous tree
Hardy to –10°F/–23°C
Part shade/regular water

This distinctive and distinguished North American native tree exhibits much of the polish and refinement of its camellia relatives. Growing at a slow to moderate rate, franklinia becomes a slender 20- to 30-foot tree with lovely, lightly striped, reddish brown bark. Large, glossy, spoon-shaped leaves are bright green through summer, scarlet in autumn. White, 3-inch single flowers—resembling camellias—appear in late summer, sometimes remaining when the leaves change color.

Culture. The same conditions that suit camellias and rhododendrons satisfy franklinia: good, well-drained, organically enriched soil on the acid side.

Good companions. *Camellia, Enkianthus, Hamamelis, Kalmia, Pieris, Rhododendron.*

❧

FUCHSIA

Fuchsia
Deciduous to semi-evergreen shrubs
Hardiness varies
Part shade/regular water

Fuchsias separate rather neatly into two general types. By far the most familiar type includes the countless varieties of *F. × hybrida*, with their summertime spectacle of flashy flowers. Less well-known are the fuchsias with smaller

blossoms on larger plants. Hardiness is what separates the two types.

As a group, the *F. × hybrida* plants are reliably hardy only to about 25°F/–4°C. Many of have lax or limber stems and are grown in hanging baskets to show off cascades of multicolored blossoms. Growing them this way also lets you move them to protection in winter if necessary. Less widely grown are shrubby, "upright" *F. × hybrida* cultivars—not because they are harder to grow but because they are usually planted in the ground, making them vulnerable to subfreezing temperatures.

The second group of fuchsias could be called relatively hardy. They don't offer the blossom size or color range of the hybrid fuchsias, but they compensate with masses of small flowers on plants that sometimes reach considerable size. Best known is *F. magellanica*, hardy to about 0°F/–18°C, although in coldest areas it may freeze to ground level and have to regrow from its roots. Normally it makes an arching shrub laden with 1½-inch purple and red flowers from late spring until frost. In mild climates, old plants may reach 20 feet high. Variant forms include one with variegated leaves.

One widely grown fuchsia, *F. tryphylla* 'Gartenmeister Bonstedt', shares some of the characteristics of each of the main types. It resembles the hardier fuchsias in the profusion of its smaller blossoms, but it has the tenderness of the *F. × hybrida* group. In mildest regions, this spreading, 2- to 3-foot shrub produces trumpet-shaped red-orange flowers throughout the year.

Culture. Success with fuchsias starts with climate. They grow best where summer is cool and the atmosphere moist.

GALAX urceolata

FUCHSIA 'Orange Queen'

The Pacific Coast offers the most suitable climates, especially where fog regularly rolls in. Where summer is warm, windy, or dry, you need to modify the environment—particularly for *F. × hybrida* plants (*F. magellanica* is less particular). Overhead sprinkling will add coolness and moisture; some gardeners install overhead mist systems that can be run by automatic controllers.

Either in containers or in the ground, give fuchsias soil that is very well-drained but liberally amended with organic matter so that it will retain moisture. In containers, you can hardly over-water fuchsias; plants in the ground need regular watering. To encourage both quantity and quality of flowers, fertilize *F. × hybrida* plants every 2 to 3 weeks (liquid formulas are easy to use).

Where winter temperatures drop low enough to kill *F. × hybrida* plants, move potted fuchsias to a cool greenhouse or indoors for the winter. Where winter lows are in the 10° to 25°F/–12° to –4°C range, protect in-ground plants with a 6-inch mound of sawdust over roots. Even if stems are killed, roots may stay alive to grow a new plant the following year.

Good companions. *Begonia, ferns, Hosta, Hydrangea, Impatiens (see "Annuals," page 60).*

❧

GALAX urceolata

Wand flower
Evergreen perennial
Hardy to –30°F/–34°C
Part to full shade/regular water

Despite the charming common name, wand flower's reputation rests on the beauty of its leaves. Slowly spreading clumps are a profusion of nearly circular 5-inch leaves with heart-shaped bases carried at the ends of long leafstalks. Glossy bright green during the growing season, leaves assume rich bronze tones over winter. Foliage grows 6 to 9 inches high, making this a good choice for planting in front-of-the-border drifts.

The midsummer flowering is a delightful bonus: 2½-foot stems carry foxtail-like spikes of tiny white flowers.

Culture. Wand flower prefers woodland conditions: high shade or dappled sunlight and acid soil amended with organic matter.

Good companions. *Clethra, Cornus, Enkianthus, Hosta, Pieris, Polygonatum, Rhododendron.*

GALIUM odoratum

Sweet woodruff
Evergreen perennial
Hardy to –20°F/–29°C
Full shade/regular water

A mass of sweet woodruff always looks fresh and cool. This lush, spreading plant has slender, 6- to 12-inch stems clothed in closely set whorls of narrow, bright green leaves. In late spring and summer, tiny 4-petaled white flowers are sprinkled over the feathery foliage surface.

GALIUM odoratum

The dried foliage of this plant is the traditional flavoring in May wine—the "sweet" part of its name. Nurseries sometimes sell sweet woodruff under its former name, *Asperula odorata.*

GAULTHERIA shallon

Culture. Regular water and a fairly good, organically amended soil will satisfy sweet woodruff. The only danger is in making it too happy—in which case sweet woodruff can become a bit invasive. Its rather shallow and noncompetitive root system makes it easy to curtail, however, and recommends it as a ground cover under a vast assortment of shade-loving plants.

Good companions. *Camellia, Enkianthus, Kalmia, Lilium, Pieris, Polygonatum, Rhododendron.*

GAULTHERIA

Gaultheria
Evergreen shrubs, ground covers
Hardiness varies
Part to full shade/regular water

These forest denizens from eastern and western North America add a touch of class to a cultivated woodsy garden. All have leathery, glossy, nearly round leaves and small, urn-shaped white or pink blossoms that form berrylike fruits.

Each species performs best within its native territory. Largest is the Pacific Coast native salal, *G. shallon,* hardy to –10°F/–23°C. Grown in shade and given regular watering, salal grows as a gradually expanding clump, becoming a handsomely irregular shrub 4 to 10 feet high. Spring flowers appear in loose 6-inch-long clusters, producing black fruits enjoyed by birds.

Two species make attractive, small-scale ground covers that spread slowly by underground stems. Taller of the two—to about 8 inches—is the western native *G. ovatifolia,* hardy to 0°F/–18°C. Its pea-

size, bright red autumn berries have a wintergreen flavor. So do those of the eastern native *G. procumbens* (hardy to –30°F/–34°C), giving it the common name wintergreen; it's also called checkerberry and teaberry. Wintergreen's foliage mass usually reaches no more than 6 inches high.

Culture. Moist, acid soil liberally amended with organic matter suits all the *Gaultheria* species.

Good companions. *Acer, Enkianthus, Fothergilla, Hamamelis, Pieris, Rhododendron.*

HALESIA

Silver bell
Deciduous trees
Hardy to –20°F/–29°C
Part shade/regular water

The two silver bells from North America can be charming components of woodland gardens where larger trees provide a backdrop and some shelter. Size is the difference between the two species.

Carolina silver bell, *H. carolina,* is smaller, growing into an arching 25- to 35-foot tree with approximately the same spread. Clusters of ½-inch, bell-shaped white flowers hang all along the branches, appearing just as leaves emerge. After blossoms fade, four-winged seed capsules form, remaining decorative after leaves have yellowed and fallen in autumn.

Mountain silver bell, *H. monticola,* may grow 60 feet high, bearing 1-inch white bells that look like clusters of cherry blossoms. Its form *H. m. rosea* has pale pink flowers that fade to white.

HALESIA carolina

Culture. The silver bells like the same conditions as rhododendrons. Give them a fairly good, acid soil that is well-drained and organically amended; mulch the soil to keep it cool, and water during dry periods.

Good companions. *Camellia, Enkianthus, Hydrangea, Leucothoe, Pieris, Rhododendron.*

❧

HAMAMELIS

Witch hazel
Deciduous shrubs
Hardiness varies
Part shade/regular water

These shrubs offer what few others do: a winter floral show. They're neither so brilliant as to call you from afar nor so subtle that they dissolve into the landscape. They simply provide heartwarming color on chill winter days.

Witch hazels are medium-size to large shrubs of spreading habit with angular or zigzag branching; some can reach tree size. Flowers consisting of numerous narrow, crumpled petals decorate bare limbs in autumn or winter, looking like blobs of shredded coconut in red, orange, or yellow. The oval leaves produce a fine color display of their own before they drop.

The most widely sold witch hazels are named selections of the hybrid *H. × intermedia* group. Generally these are large shrubs to about 15 feet high, hardy to –20°F/–29°C.

Chinese witch hazel, *H. mollis,* is hardy to –10°F/–23°C. Fragrant yellow flowers decorate this widely spreading,

HAMAMELIS × intermedia 'Diane'

HEDERA helix 'Buttercup'

12-foot shrub, which can be trained as a small tree perhaps twice that tall. Japanese witch hazel, *H. japonica,* is a shorter plant with smaller flowers, hardy to –20°F/–29°C. Bright red autumn foliage sets it apart.

Two North American species are hardy to –20°F/–29°C. The small, fragrant yellow flowers of *H. vernalis* come soon after the new year; plants are upright to about 10 feet, with equal spread. The yellow blossoms of *H. virginiana,* an open shrub about 15 feet tall and wide, usually appear when the leaves turn yellow in autumn.

Culture. Give witch hazels a fairly good soil, neutral to acid, enriched with organic matter. If you need to shape plants, winter is a good time to do so: you can use the prunings for bouquets.

Good companions. *Buxus, Enkianthus, Ilex, Kalmia, Leucothoe, Pieris, Rhododendron.*

❧

HEDERA

Ivy
Evergreen vines
Hardiness varies
Part to full shade/moderate to regular water

Depending on your experience, you may consider ivy either the perfect vine/ground cover or the peskiest. Once established, ivy is virtually unstoppable. Ground-cover plants will climb up onto any vertical surface their aerial rootlets encounter: walls and fences, trees, flower pots, garden furniture. Plants grown to

cover vertical surfaces will spread out onto the ground, too, if not curbed.

These cautionary notes don't mean "stay away." You can turn such tenacity to your advantage. Ivy will transform any unattractive wire fence into a solid wall of handsome foliage. Planted as a ground cover, its roots fill soil densely and deeply—especially important on erosion-prone slopes.

Old, vertical plants stop vining and produce shrubby, branching stems that bear tiny greenish flower clusters followed by berrylike black fruits—and volunteer ivy plants if birds eat and scatter them.

English ivy, *H. helix,* is hardy to 0°F/–18°C; a few selections survive to –10°F/–23°C. This is the familiar ivy with dark green, matte-finish leaves veined lighter. Leaves are 2 to 4 inches wide, each with 3 to 5 lobes. Nurseries may offer selections with yellow, cream, or white foliage variegation. Specialists carry more variants, including some with smaller or differently-shaped leaves.

Algerian ivy, *H. canariensis,* is hardy to 10°F/–12°C. Leaves are notably glossy and may reach 8 inches across. The widely-planted form 'Variegata' adds broad creamy white margins.

Culture. Ivy is not especially fussy about soil, but a bit of preparation ensures a good start. For just one or a few plants, add a generous amount of organic matter to the soil in the planting hole. If you will be planting many rooted cuttings for ground cover, liberally amend the soil of the entire area, digging in organic matter 8 to 12 inches deep. To lessen the chance of planting fatalities, thoroughly moisten roots and stems first, and set plants into moist soil.

Water regularly to get plants well established. Thereafter, give Algerian ivy regular watering; English ivy needs regular watering in hot-summer regions but tolerates moderate watering elsewhere.

Ground cover plantings will build up a thick thatch of stems after several years.

HELLEBORUS niger

Shear back to near ground level or mow with a heavy-duty mower.

Good companions. *Acer, Camellia, Fatsia, Myrtus, Pittosporum, Podocarpus, Taxus.*

❧ HELLEBORUS

Hellebore
Deciduous and evergreen perennials
Hardiness varies
Part to full shade/regular water

The various hellebores are fine foliage plants that also happen to bear elegant flowers. Plants are mounds of bold foliage, each leaf consisting of large, leathery leaflets arranged like fingers on an outstretched hand. All hellebores have flowers of wild-rose simplicity in winter and early spring.

Two species make foliage clumps to about 1½ feet high, the leafstalks rising directly from the ground. Christmas rose, *H. niger,* is hardy to –30°F/–34°C and needs some winter chill to perform well. White, 2-inch flowers come one per stem, sometimes as early as December. Lenten rose, *H. orientalis,* is also hardy to –30°F/–34°C but will grow well in mild-winter regions. In late winter or early spring, branched clusters bear flowers of white, pink, or brownish purple, often with dark spots in the center.

Two other species differ by sending up leafy stems from the ground, bearing dome-shaped blossom clusters at the tips. After flowering, stems die down as new ones replace them. The hardier of the two species, to –10°F/–23°C, is *H. foetidus.* Its narrow leaflets are blackish green, the backdrop for inch-wide green flowers on 1½-foot-high stems in late

winter and early spring. Corsican helle-bore, *H. lividus corsicus,* is hardy to –5°F/–21°C. Its stems may reach 3 feet, carrying rather pale blue-green foliage and pale chartreuse blossoms that can come as early as autumn in mild regions, from winter to early spring in chillier areas.

Culture. All hellebores appreciate good, organically amended soil, regular water-ing, and light shade or dappled sunlight. Established plants of *H. foetidus* and *H. lividus corsicus* will prosper with just moderate watering.

Good companions. *Brunnera, Dicentra, Digitalis, Epimedium, Polygonatum.*

❧ HEMEROCALLIS

Daylily
Deciduous and evergreen perennials
Hardiness varies
Part shade/regular water

A staple perennial for sunny gardens, daylilies also thrive in partial shade with only a little loss of bloom production. They offer a dazzling range of colors on plants from foot-high miniatures to 4- and 5-foot goliaths. Each plant is a spray of cornlike leaves; a clump is truly a fountain of foliage.

Blossoms are lily- to chalice-shaped— either single, like a lily, or double with multiple segments. Though individual blooms last but a day, a stem contains enough buds to give a prolonged display. Modern hybrids have not only a great color range but also flowers that are more durable than old-fashioned kinds;

HEMEROCALLIS fulva

many can remain open well into the evening or even the next morning.

Flowering starts in mid- to late spring and can last well over a month; some kinds provide a scattering of flowers over summer. Reblooming types will mount another display in late summer to midautumn.

Deciduous daylilies are hardy to about –35°F/–37°C but may not be totally successful in frost-free regions. Evergreen kinds usually need winter pro-tection where tem-peratures drop below –20°F/–29°C; the semi-evergreen plants may also ben-efit from it.

Culture. Tough and adaptable, daylilies nevertheless give their best show in good, well-drained, organically enriched soil. Water regularly during dry periods. When planting in partial shade, remember that flowers will face the light.

× *HEUCHERELLA tiarelloides*

Good companions. *Alchemilla, Bergen-ia, Filipendula, Hypericum, Platycodon.*

❧ × HEUCHERELLA tiarelloides

Heucherella
Evergreen perennial
Hardy to –20°F/–29°C
Part shade/regular water

Sun-loving coral bells (*Heuchera*) crossed with shade-dwelling foam flower (*Tiarella cordifolia*) produced this small group of clump-forming perennials well suited for light shade or dappled sun-light. Most commonly sold is 'Bridget Bloom', which produces foot-high, airy spikes of small, starlike pink flowers in the manner of *Heuchera.* The lobed 3½-inch leaves take after the *Tiarella* parent.

HOSTA

Culture. Plant in well-drained, organically amended soil. See that plants have regular moisture during dry periods.

Good companions. *Hosta, Iris foetidissima, Lamium, Lilium, Platycodon, Polygonatum, Tricyrtis.*

❧
HOSTA

Hosta, plantain lily, funkia
Deciduous perennials
Hardy to −35°F/−37°C
Part to full shade/regular water

Most hostas do produce flowers, but it is their wonderfully ornamental foliage that catches your attention. Leaves may be lance-shaped, heart-shaped, oval, or nearly round—always carried at the ends of leafstalks rising directly from the ground. The leaves generally radiate from a tight clump in an overlapping mound of foliage.

Leaves may be smooth or quiltlike or puckery, with a glossy surface or a grayish, plumlike bloom; and their margins may be smooth or gracefully undulated. You'll find great variety in leaf color, too: light to dark green to chartreuse, gray, and blue. Many variegations in white, yellow, or green are available.

Plants run from no higher than 3 inches to showpiece specimens 3 feet high and wide. Flowers come in white, lilac, and violet—bell-shaped to lilylike in form, hanging or outward-facing on spikes that barely top the foliage in some species or rise well above it in others.

Culture. Hostas are no challenge where frosty to freezing winters are followed by humid summers, cool or warm. The best growth comes in good, organically

enriched soil kept well-watered. For the most luxuriant foliage, fertilize plants when new leaves appear in spring.

Good companions. *Alchemilla, Anemone, Astilbe, Campanula, Dicentra, Polygonatum, Thalictrum.*

❧
HYDRANGEA

Hydrangea
Deciduous shrubs and vine
Hardiness varies
Part to full shade/regular water

The familiar "mop-head" hydrangea (*H. macrophylla*) sets the tone for the various species: big leaves, big flower clusters, big shrubs.

These eye-catching plants have two kinds of flowers: tiny, starlike fertile blossoms and (the major display) sterile flowers with petal-like sepals. The showiest kinds contain only sterile flowers in their blossom clusters. Another variation, however, features sterile flowers ringing a cluster of fertile ones in "lace-cap" formation. All hydrangeas flower in summer, often into autumn. The sterile blossoms can remain colorful for many weeks before they fade attractively to dull pink or green.

Bigleaf hydrangea, *H. macrophylla*, is hardy to −10°F/−23°C. Typical plants reach 4 to 8 feet high and wide and can bear blossom clusters a foot across. Glossy, 8-inch leaves are in scale. A great number of named selections exist—both with all-sterile flowers (sometimes called "hortensias") and with lace-cap clusters—but nurseries often sell them simply by color: white, blue, pink, raspberry red. French hybrids (the same kind you find in florist shops) make smaller plants to about 4 feet high.

Oakleaf hydrangea, *H. quercifolia*, also is hardy to −10°F/−23°C. Its large, lobed leaves change in autumn to a bronzy red. This is a clump-forming shrub, with numerous stems rising from the ground up to 6 feet high. The 10-inch, cone-shaped clusters of white flow-

ers combine fertile and sterile blossoms; the selection 'Snow Queen' offers virtually all-sterile flowers.

Two species take winters to −30°F/−34°C. Smooth hydrangea, *H. arborescens,* may reach 10 feet high, bearing lace-cap or all-fertile flowers. The selection 'Grandiflora' (often called "hills-of-snow") offers 6-inch snowball-like clusters of sterile flowers on a 4-foot plant; 'Annabelle' is similar but has clusters twice as big. The old favorite peegee hydrangea, *H. paniculata* 'Grandiflora', will grow as a rounded shrub 15 feet high or can be trained into tree form (with one or several trunks) to perhaps 25 feet. Its 12- to 15-inch-long spikes of sterile flowers look like large white lilacs. Leaves turn bronze in autumn before they drop.

HYDRANGEA macrophylla 'Tricolor'

Climbing hydrangea, *H. anomala petiolaris (H. petiolaris)*, is hardy to −20°F/−29°C. Like ivy, it can climb to great heights by means of tenacious aerial rootlets; and, like ivy, it sends out shrubby side branches that produce flowers—in this case, white lace-cap clusters to 10 inches across.

Culture. To support their lush growth, hydrangeas need good, well-drained soil and regular watering. They benefit from some annual pruning: heavier to encourage larger blossoms, lighter to emphasize larger plants.

Good companions. *Acer, Buxus, Franklinia, Helleborus, Hosta, Pittosporum, Stewartia.*

HYPERICUM calycinum

HYPERICUM

St. Johnswort
Evergreen shrubs and ground cover
Hardiness varies
Part shade/moderate to regular water

Yellow is St. Johnswort's color, displayed in five-petaled flowers that resemble single roses. With one exception, this summer cheer is dispensed on upright to arching plants in the 2- to 6-foot height range; oval or elongated leaves grow in opposite pairs along the stems.

The hardiest shrubby species is *H. frondosum*—to –10°F/–23°C. It also has the smallest blossoms (to 1½ inches across) and loses some of its leaves in the coldest winters. Three shrubby St. Johnsworts take temperatures down to 0°F/–18°C and bear flowers in the 2- to 3-inch category: *H. beanii (H. patulum henryi), H. 'Hidcote' (H. patulum 'Hidcote')*, and *H. kouytchense* (including the plant sold as *H. 'Sungold'*). Least cold-tolerant (to 10°F/–12°C) is *H. 'Rowallane'*, an upright, rather sparse plant with sumptuous 3-inch blossoms.

Creeping St. Johnswort or Aaron's beard, *H. calycinum,* makes a dense, virtually indestructible ground cover hardy to 0°F/–18°C. Plants spread aggressively by underground stems, sending up arching branches that form an even cover about 12 inches high. Though this plant is considered invasive in some situations, its intertwined mat of roots and stems holds its own with tree roots and helps prevent erosion on slopes.

Culture. These are adaptable plants, unfussy about soil and persisting with only moderate watering. For best performance, though, give them average to good soil, well-drained, and regular watering in dry periods. Shrubby types look best in regions where some atmospheric moisture is the norm.

Good companions. *Aegopodium, Aspidistra, Berberis, Buxus, Mahonia, Osmanthus, Rubus.*

ILEX

Holly
Deciduous and evergreen shrubs
Hardiness varies
Part shade/regular water

Holly is, of course, the familiar holiday symbol with its red berries and spiny leaves. But hollies are a varied lot—including plants that have smooth leaves, some that have no berries, and others that drop their foliage to show off their berries in splendid isolation. Leaves come in shades of green or variegated in white, cream, or yellow. Besides red berries, you can find orange, yellow, white, and black.

Hollies are shrubby plants by nature, but many an old specimen can be seen rising fully to tree height—though usually carrying branches all the way to the ground like an overgrown shrub. Among plants that ultimately become trees is the classic English holly, *I. aquifolium*— but it, like other tree-size species, is also available in named selections that remain shrubby. There are even extra-dwarf hollies that grow no higher than 1½ feet.

Most holly plants are either male or female, and the bright berries come only on female plants. Although a few hollies will bear fruits without pollination, the rule is that for berry production you need both male and female plants growing close enough for pollination to take place. The easy solution is to plant a male of the same species as the females; if you plant a different species, berries will form only if both species flower at the same time.

One male plant will pollinate up to 10 nearby females. Nurseries carry named male selections for planting as pollinators; some growers offer female plants with a male branch grafted onto them to guarantee berry set with just the one plant.

The hardiest species is the deciduous winterberry, *I. verticillata,* which takes temperatures down to –30°F/–34°C; in warmer regions, it puts on a good show of yellow autumn leaf color. Among evergreen kinds, blue holly, *I. × meserveae,* and American holly, *I. opaca,* are hardy to –20°F/–29°C. Both have spiny leaves and are available in various named selections. Japanese holly, *I. crenata,* is hardy to –10°F/–23°C. Its small, oval leaves could nearly pass for boxwood, and like boxwood it is a good hedge plant.

A number of evergreen hollies will take temperatures to 0°F/–18°C—among them the "typical" red-berried/spiny-leafed types and all possible foliage and fruit variations. Included are English holly, *I. aquifolium*; its hybrids *I. × altaclarensis* (particularly the selection 'Wilsonii') and *I. × aquipernyi*; and Chinese holly, *I. cornuta.* The maverick in this hardiness group is yaupon, *I. vomitoria.* Its leaves are small, narrow,

ILEX verticillata

and wavy-edged, while the tiny berries come without a pollenizer.

Culture. Hollies are easy to grow and respond to good culture: fertile, well-drained, slightly acid soil, and regular watering during dry periods. *I. vomitoria* will grow in alkaline soil and tolerate some drought.

Mulch plants to conserve soil moisture. For the most berries, locate plants where they get plenty of light; fruit production decreases as shade increases.

Good companions. *Camellia, Enkianthus, Franklinia, Halesia, Pieris, Rhododendron.*

❧

IRIS foetidissima

Gladwin iris
Evergreen perennial
Hardy to 0°F/–18°C
Part to full shade/moderate to regular water

From its overall appearance, you can recognize this plant as an iris. But in several details it is atypical. The glossy, dark green leaves are evergreen and always attractive; clumps gradually increase in size and beauty but can remain in place indefinitely.

In mid-spring, flower stalks grow 1½ to 2 feet tall; blossoms mingle blue-gray and dull tan—subtly attractive but hardly showy. The gherkin-size seed capsules, however, provide real color impact when they break open to reveal bright orange-scarlet seeds that remain attached to the pods rather than falling to the ground.

With a bit of searching, you may find selections with yellow or lavender-blue flowers or white-variegated foliage.

Culture. This is a totally undemanding plant. You can give it good soil and ordinary garden watering, or place it in poor soil and deep shade, letting rain nurture established plants.

IRIS foetidissima

JUNIPERUS chinensis

Good companions. *Bergenia, Cyclamen, Helleborus, Lamium, Myosotis, Vancouveria.*

❧

JUNIPERUS

Juniper
Evergreen shrubs
Hardiness varies
Part shade/moderate water

Juniper is the ubiquitous and virtually all-purpose evergreen. Its virtues sometimes go unappreciated simply because it is common. In one species or another, juniper will grow almost anywhere. Various common names bear this out—shore juniper, Waukegan juniper, Hollywood juniper, alligator juniper, Utah juniper. So do such cultivar names as 'San Jose', 'Bar Harbor', 'Calgary Carpet', and 'Wichita Blue'.

You can find junipers that spread widely and hug the ground or form a tight carpet 1 to 3 feet high. Others are shrubby, splaying branches out like a fountain, growing upright, or twisting picturesquely. Columnar forms run from fat pencils to tubby pillars, while some tree junipers grow 50 feet tall.

Junipers offer a range of foliage colors, including silvery blue, blue-gray, blue-green, and bright green; some plants have chartreuse or yellow new growth or creamy yellow variegation. Foliage may consist of small, prickly needles (juvenile foliage); tiny overlapping scales (mature foliage); or both needles and scales on the same plant.

Ground cover and shrub junipers are best for shaded gardens. Tree and columnar types may become unattractively sparse or leggy in shade. Ground cover and shrubby junipers are all selected forms of these species: *J. chinensis* (hardy to –30°F/–34°C), *J. communis* (hardy to –40°F/–40°C), *J. sabina* (hardy to –30°F/–34°C), *J. scopulorum* (hardy to –20°F/–29°C), *J. squamata* (hardy to –20°F/–29°C), and *J. virginiana* (hardy to –40°F/–40°C).

Culture. Junipers are not particular about soil: they'll grow well in light and heavy soils, acid and alkaline. What they don't handle well is overly wet soil. Water moderately during dry periods; and in a high-rainfall region, plant in soil that drains well.

Good companions. *Arbutus, Aucuba, Berberis, Euonymus, Laurus, Mahonia, Myrtus, Rhamnus.*

❧

KALMIA latifolia

Mountain laurel, calico bush
Evergreen shrub
Hardy to –20°F/–29°C
Part shade/regular water

This rhododendron relative is one of the true gems among native North American shrubs. Rounded bushes eventually reach 10 feet or more in height and spread, clothed in handsome, leathery, long leaves that are dark green on top, yellowish green beneath.

Even the clustered blossoms suggest rhododendron, except that each long flower stalk bears a 1-inch, chalice-shaped flower with five starlike points. Pink is the standard color, but blossoms often show a subtly different shade in their throats and may have contrasting stamens.

Specialty nurseries offer an increasing range of named selections, with flowers from white through various pinks to red—some with contrasting color bands. 'Elf' is a small-growing selection just 3 feet high and 5 feet wide.

Culture. Give mountain laurel the same garden location and care you would rhododendrons. Plant in well-drained, acid soil enriched with organic matter, then mulch beneath plants for coolness and water retention. Give regular water during dry periods.

Like rhododendrons, mountain laurels have their favorite climates, eschewing hot and dry weather. The best regions are the Pacific Northwest and the eastern states—westward into the Mississippi Valley, excluding Florida and the Gulf Coast.

Good companions. *Epimedium, Franklinia, Halesia, Leucothoe, Rhododendron, Vancouveria.*

KALMIA latifolia

❧

KERRIA japonica

Kerria
Deciduous shrub
Hardy to –20°F/–29°C
Part shade/moderate to regular water

In all seasons, kerria offers visual appeal. Springtime brings on vibrant, yolk-yellow flowers. In summer, the gracefully arching, 6- to 8-foot plant is a mound of bright green, texture-veined leaves—which turn yellow come autumn. In winter, the plant attracts attention for its leaf-green bare stems.

The basic species bears 5-petaled, single flowers that resemble small roses scattered over the leaves. More widely grown, however, is the selection 'Pleniflora', which has inch-wide, many-petaled blossoms that are considerably longer-lasting than the single flowers. Other selections include plants with variegated leaves (yellow or white) and variegated stems.

Culture. Kerria thrives in good soil with regular watering, but such ideal conditions encourage rank growth at the expense of flowers. A better display comes in just average soil with moderate water. Allow enough space for the slender stems to arch and mound freely; a plant cut back to fit a restricted space loses much of its charm.

Good companions. *Acanthus, Aucuba, Hemerocallis, Osmanthus, Taxus.*

❧

LAMIUM

Dead nettle
Deciduous to evergreen perennials
Hardy to –20°F/–29°C
Full shade/regular to frequent water

Dead nettle's silver-variegated foliage adds a bright sparkle to shaded locations.

Spotted nettle, *L. maculatum,* is a spreading ground cover that rises to about 6 inches and extends 2 to 3 feet across. The basic species has clustered pink flowers over silver-marked, gray-green leaves, but named selections offer superior leaf and flower combinations. These include 'Beacon Silver' and 'White Nancy' (green-edged silver leaves with, respectively, pink and white flowers), and pink-flowered 'Checquers' (green leaf with white median stripe).

Yellow archangel, *L. galeobdolon* (sometimes sold as *Lamiastrum galeob-*

LAMIUM maculatum 'White Nancy'

KERRIA japonica

dolon), makes slowly spreading clumps to 1½ feet high; the small yellow flowers are insignificant. The selection 'Variegatum' has silver leaves elaborately veined in green; 'Herman's Pride' is lower-growing and features silver-flecked, dark green leaves.

Culture. Plant dead nettles in ordinary garden soil, and give them regular watering. They need a steady moisture supply, especially in warm climates, where plants can wilt if soil is dry. The two basic species can be somewhat invasive under best growing conditions, but the named selections are less rampant. In all but mildest-winter areas, plants die back to the ground in winter.

Good companions. *Aspidistra, Anemone, Bergenia, Digitalis, Lilium, Platycodon.*

❧

LAURUS nobilis

Sweet bay, Grecian laurel
Evergreen tree or shrub
Hardy to 10°F/–12°C
Part shade/moderate water

Sweet bay—source of both the culinary bay leaf and the "crown of laurels" in antiquity—offers virtually nothing but foliage, but it does that quite well. Its characteristically aromatic leaves are leathery, glossy, pointed ovals to 4 inches long, and they densely cover a broadly conical plant that always looks neat. In time, sweet bay will produce clusters of insignificant yellow flowers followed by purplish black, 1-inch berries.

You can use sweet bay as a rather formal accent plant in a large container, set out a number of plants to serve as a hedge or screen, or simply let one plant

LAURUS nobilis

LIGULARIA stenocephala 'The Rocket'

grow—allowing it to eventually graduate from shrub to tree perhaps as tall as 40 feet. The selection 'Saratoga' is inherently more treelike.

Culture. Sweet bay is not particular about soil but does need good drainage. Established plants withstand prolonged dry periods but will take moderate to regular watering as long as the soil doesn't stay saturated.

Good companions. *Acanthus, Berberis, Hedera, Juniperus, Mahonia, Myrtus, Rubus.*

❧
LEUCOTHOE fontanesiana

Drooping leucothoe
Evergreen shrub
Hardy to –20°F/–29°C
Part to full shade/regular water

This elegant rhododendron relative hails from the woods of eastern North America. For years it was known as *Leucothoe catesbaei*, and some nurseries still sell it by that name. Its slowly spreading clumps consist of arching stems 2 to 6 feet long, each bearing opposing ranks of polished, 6-inch oval leaves. In spring and summer, foliage is dark green; but in autumn the color changes to a bronzy purple that lasts

LEUCOTHOE fontanesiana

throughout winter. Drooping clusters of small, creamy white blossoms (shaped like lily-of-the-valley flowers) bedeck the stems in mid- to late spring.

Two foliage variants offer changes from basic green: leaves of 'Rainbow' combine green with cream, yellow, and pink; 'Scarletta' has bronze-purple leaves all year.

Culture. Give drooping leucothoe well-drained, organically-enriched, somewhat acid soil, and see that moisture is available during dry periods.

Good companions. *Acer, Enkianthus, Epimedium, Halesia, Ilex, Kalmia, Rhododendron, Stewartia.*

❧
LIGULARIA

Ligularia
Deciduous perennials
Hardy to –30°F/–34°C except as noted
Part shade/regular to frequent water

Given rich soil and plenty of water, the ligularias make a dramatic landscape statement. Hefty clumps display long-stalked leaves that usually are heart-shaped or nearly circular in outline and a foot or more across. Their margins may be strongly toothed, waved, even deeply dissected in the manner of some Japanese maples. With such foliage magnificence, it may come as a surprise that the flowers are yellow to orange daisies!

You can recognize *L. dentata* by its flattened flowers clusters on 3- to 5-foot stems above wavy-edged round leaves. 'Desdemona' and 'Othello', with purple-infused leaves, are the most commonly sold selections. All but one of the other standard ligularias bear small flowers in upright spikes 5 to 6 feet tall. These include *L. przewalskii, L. stenocephala* (and its selection or hybrid 'The Rocket'), *L. wilsoniana*, and *L.* 'Gregynog Gold'. The exception is *L. tussilaginea*, the leopard plant. Its yellow daisies come in clusters of a few flowers just above rubbery kidney-shaped to nearly circular leaves on 1- to 2-foot leafstalks. The

widely sold selection 'Aureo-maculata' has dark green leaves spattered in creamy white.

Culture. Good, organically enriched soil is a must for ligularia success. Combine this with ample water for the most impressive growth. These are good plants alongside ponds and streams.

Good companions. *Aruncus, Astilbe, Cimicifuga, Filipendula, Trollius .*

❧
LILIUM

Lily
Bulbs
Hardiness varies
Part shade/regular water

The world of lilies is vast and enchanting, including foot-tall species possessed of a wildflower charm as well as elegant 8-foot-high plants striking enough to stop traffic. The color range is equally wide: yellow, orange, red, maroon, pink, cream, white, lilac, purple, pale green, and multicolor combinations.

Despite such variety, lilies all conform to a general pattern. Bulbs consist of overlapping scales: think of a head of

LILIUM 'Imperial Gold'

garlic with rather flattened cloves. From each bulb grows a vertical stem clothed in narrow leaves and terminating in a single flower or a branched cluster of blossoms. The six-segmented flowers may be chalice-shaped, wide open, or with segments recurved—always with prominent stamens. All the flowers of an individual plant face the same way—down, out, or up.

LIRIOPE muscari 'Variegata'

Most lilies grown today are hybrids developed in this century from diverse species. These hybrids not only offer floral qualities improved over their wild ancestors, but also greater health and vigor—in other words, they are easier to grow. Catalogs of lily specialists list a dazzling array of hybrids and some species, a diversity that has been subdivided into nine "Divisions," eight of them based on hybrid ancestry and the ninth including all species.

The hardiest hybrid types (Asiatic, Martagon, and Aurelian hybrids) take temperatures to around −30°F/−34°C; the Candidum, Longiflorum, and Oriental hybrids are hardy to around -20°F/−9°C. American hybrids come from diverse ancestries, so their hardiness ranges from −10° to −30°F/−23° to −34°C.

Culture. Lilies have three basic needs: soil that is fertile, well-drained, loose, and deep; ample moisture all year (except for Candidum hybrids and various species); and coolness and shade at ground level but more light for stems and blossoms. While they will grow in full sun where summers are cool, foggy, or overcast, in most other climates lilies like filtered sunlight, high shade (but plenty of light), or morning sun/afternoon light shade.

Plant in a wind-sheltered location so that plants will stay upright without staking. Before planting, incorporate plenty of organic matter deeply into the soil. Mulch the planting with 2 to 3 inches of organic matter to conserve moisture and keep soil cool.

Good companions. *Alchemilla, Brunnera, Corydalis, Dicentra, ferns, Galax, Hosta.*

❧

LIRIOPE & OPHIOPOGON

Lily turf
Evergreen perennials
Hardy to −10°F/−23°C except as noted
Part to full shade/regular water

Although these two similar plants do produce attractive flowers, they are grown primarily for their foliage. Fountainlike clumps of glossy, nearly grassy leaves make handsome accent clumps, pathway-border plants, and even small-scale ground covers. Small blossoms come in tight spikes atop vertical stems, either above the foliage or among the leaves.

The most widely grown is big blue lily turf, *Liriope muscari*. Its foliage clumps reach about 1½ feet high; the midsummer blossoms are dark violet and barely top the leaves. Named selections offer different flower colors, larger foliage, and several variegated-leaf versions, including 8-inch-tall 'Silvery Midget'. Creeping lily turf, *L. spicata*, makes a dense and widely spreading ground cover of dark, grassy leaves to 9 inches high; 'Silver Dragon' is a white-variegated form.

Closely related *Ophiopogon jaburan* often is sold as *Liriope gigantea*. Its dark green leaves can reach 3 feet in length; plants are hardy just to 10°F/−12°C. White flowers partially hidden in the foliage are followed by decorative metallic blue fruits. The variegated leaves of the form 'Vittatus' become entirely green by midsummer.

Mondo grass, *O. japonicus,* is another nearly grasslike ground cover growing about 12 inches high, but it is less vigorous than the similar creeping lily turf, described previously. Pale lilac flowers produce blue fruits; plants are hardy just to 10°F/−12°C.

Culture. The lily turfs need only average soil that drains well. They'll get by with moderate water, but they look better if they are watered during dry periods.

Good companions. *Acanthus, Anemone, Aspidistra, Hosta, Polygonatum, Tricyrtis.*

❧

LONICERA

Honeysuckle
Deciduous to evergreen vines
Hardiness varies
Part shade/regular water

Vigor and fragrance typify most honeysuckles. These are easy-to-grow vines that, despite individual differences, share a general pattern. Tube-shaped flowers come in clusters, and oval leaves (often a bluish green) are in opposite pairs on flexible stems that climb by twining.

LONICERA × brownii 'Dropmore Scarlet'

Scarlet trumpet honeysuckle, *L. × brownii,* is semideciduous and hardy to −40°F/−40°C. Firecracker red (but scentless) flowers appear in summer on a restrained vine growing to about 10 feet; 'Dropmore Scarlet' is a superior selection. Gold flame honeysuckle, *L. heckrottii,* is partly to totally deciduous and hardy to −10°F/−23°C. Blue-green leaves cover a modest vine growing to about 15 feet; pink buds from spring to frost open

LYSIMACHIA nummularia

to flowers that are coral-colored outside, yellow within.

A bit farther-reaching, to around 20 feet, is woodbine, *L. periclymenum.* Evergreen in mild climates, it becomes progressively deciduous as it approaches its hardiness limit of –10°F/–23°C. Fragrant blossoms in summer and autumn produce a conspicuous crop of red berries. Superior named selections include 'Serotina', with flowers of purple and yellow; 'Serotina Florida', with flowers of red and cream; and 'Berries Jubilee', with yellow blossoms. The creamy white flowers of 'Graham Thomas' come on a much more extensive vine, to about 40 feet.

Trumpet honeysuckle, *L. sempervirens,* is evergreen to semideciduous, hardy to about –20°F/–29°C. The scentless, orange-yellow to scarlet flowers appear in summer on a vine that may reach 20 feet. Scarlet fruits come later.

Culture. Honeysuckles flourish in average soil with some watering during dry periods.

Good companions. *Buxus, Euonymus, Hydrangea, Hypericum, Osmanthus, Rhaphiolepis, Viburnum.*

LYSIMACHIA nummularia

Creeping Jenny, moneywort
Evergreen perennial
Hardy to –30°F/–34°C
Part to full shade/regular to
frequent water

Given favorable conditions, this earth-hugging ground cover does more than

creep—it fairly runs. In a small space, creeping Jenny might be called invasive; but where its expansionist tendencies can be an asset—under shrubs and among larger perennials, for example—it will become an appreciated lush carpet of light green.

The nearly round leaves are less than an inch across, clothing spreading stems that root where leaf nodes contact moist soil. In summer, this green mat becomes dotted with inch-wide, bright yellow flowers. The yellow-leafed form 'Aurea' adds a particularly bright touch to shaded areas.

Culture. Shade and moist soil are all it takes to encourage creeping Jenny. In fact, this plant will thrive in soil that is continually damp.

Good companions. *Aconitum, Astilbe, Carex* (see "Ornamental Grasses," page 78), *Clethra, ferns, Hosta, Tricyrtis.*

MAHONIA

Mahonia
Evergreen shrubs
Hardiness varies
Part shade/moderate to regular water

Handsome and durable foliage distinguishes all mahonias. Closely related to barberries *(Berberis)* and classified among them by some botanists, they show the connection only in their clusters of small, bright yellow blossoms. Mahonia foliage shares a characteristic with another relative, *Nandina*: what appear to be individual leaves are actual-

MAHONIA bealei

ly leaflets of larger compound leaves. Some mahonias become branching shrubs, but several species form clumps of upright, unbranched stems—much like nandina.

Details vary among the species, but spiny or prickly leaflet margins are typical. Conspicuous clusters of blossoms at branch tips are followed by berrylike blue-black or reddish fruits.

Oregon grape, *M. aquifolium,* is the most widely grown species, hardy to –10°F/–23°C. The "grape" name comes from dark fruits with a chalky surface "bloom"; the name "aquifolium" refers to the leaflets, which nearly duplicate English holly leaves. Foliage emerges light bronze, matures to medium or dark green, then becomes bronzy purple over winter in colder regions. Stems rise from the ground—some upright, some spreading—to form a plant that increases in bulk over time as new stems grow up, reaching 6 feet or more in height.

The selection 'Compacta' grows no higher than 2 feet, spreading by underground stems into sizeable patches. Hybrid *M.* 'Golden Abundance' is similar to Oregon grape but more dense, with more flowers and fruits.

The California holly grape, *M. pinnata,* also resembles Oregon grape but with wavy-edged, spinier leaves, brighter new growth, and a 10-foot potential height; plants are hardy just to 10°F/–12°C.

Longleaf mahonia, *M. nervosa,* is hardy to about –10°F/–23°C. Growth usually is low, to about 2 feet, and plants spread into patches by underground stems. With its 12- to 18-inch leaves composed of opposing pairs of hollylike leaflets, longleaf mahonia looks rather like a coarse, spiny fern. Upright clusters of yellow blossoms yield blue berries.

Leatherleaf mahonia, *M. bealei,* is a living sculpture—a clump of almost vertical stems crowned by whorls of horizontal leaves. Each leaf is over a foot long, consisting of 7 to 15 yellow-green, oval, spiny leaflets. Spikes of yellow blossoms are followed by chalky blue berries.

Plants reach 10 to 12 feet tall and are hardy to 0°F/–18°C.

Culture. All but leatherleaf mahonia will grow in virtually any soil and thrive on just moderate watering. Leatherleaf mahonia needs fairly good, organically enriched soil and supplemental watering to keep soil moist.

Good companions. *Acer, Berberis, Buxus, Cercis, Juniperus, Podocarpus, Taxus.*

❧ MERTENSIA

Bluebells
Deciduous perennials
Hardy to –35°F/–37°C
Part to full shade/regular water

MERTENSIA virginica

The bluebells are a harbinger of spring. Clear blue blossoms, nodding and shaped like elongated bells, proclaim the start of the season.

Virginia bluebells, *M. virginica,* is the more readily available of the two North American species. Broadly oval bluish green leaves on 2-foot stems grow in loose clumps. At the ends of stems hang clusters of inch-long, trumpet-shaped flowers that open from pinkish buds.

Mountain bluebells, *M. ciliata,* may reach 3 feet high, bearing slightly smaller blossoms with fringed petal margins.

MYOSOTIS scorpioides

Both begin to die down after flowering, Virginia bluebells becoming dormant by midsummer and mountain bluebells staying green longer if well watered.

Culture. Woodland soil—organically enriched and rather loose—is the bluebells' preference. Give them plenty of moisture from the time growth begins until flowering finishes. You can decrease watering after plants have died down, but never let soil go totally dry.

Good companions. *Dicentra, Doronicum, ferns, Hosta, Primula, Pulmonaria, Trillium, Trollius.*

❧ MYOSOTIS scorpioides

Forget-me-not
Deciduous to evergreen perennial
Hardy to –20°F/–29°C
Part to full shade/regular water

The forget-me-not's small flowers of purest light blue illuminate shaded gardens with an azure haze in spring and summer. Carried in elongated, curving clusters, these sparkling, yellow-centered blossoms rise above 6- to 12-inch-high plants covered in narrow bright green leaves. You can find pink and white forms, too.

Unlike its annual kin *Myosotis sylvatica* (see page 61), this perennial forget-me-not spreads by creeping roots and can be used as a modest ground cover.

Culture. Forget-me-not needs only organically amended soil, always moist but not saturated. In the colder range of

its adaptability, plants will die down over winter and reappear in spring.

Good companions. *Aspidistra, Bergenia, Clethra, Digitalis, Hosta, Lilium, Polygonatum.*

❧ MYRTUS communis

Myrtle
Evergreen shrub
Hardy to 15°F/–9°C
Part shade/moderate to regular water

This plant of classical antiquity is intimately associated with Mediterranean gardens. And though it will flourish in Mediterranean-style sun and heat, it is perfectly at home in partial or light shade.

At all times of year, myrtle looks fresh and healthy, thanks to its plentiful glossy foliage. Each leaf is lance-shaped, to 2 inches long, and aromatic when crushed. In summer this neat and tidy backdrop is liberally sprinkled with small white flowers that will be followed, in time, by pea-size black fruits. Plants are naturally rounded, rather billowy if not sheared, to about 6 feet high and wide. Very old plants may become picturesquely gnarled shrub-trees.

MYRTUS communis

Named selections offer variegated foliage, smaller plants, a boxwood mimic ('Buxifolia'), and a plant with upright branches and upward-pointing foliage ('Boetica').

Culture. Myrtle is a rugged, easy-to-grow shrub suitable for seashore, desert, and all points between. Plants prefer well-drained soil but are not otherwise particular. When established, myrtle can grow with little or no supplemental watering.

Good companions. *Acanthus, Arbutus, Hedera, Juniperus, Laurus, Mahonia, Rhamnus.*

❧ NANDINA *domestica*

Heavenly bamboo, nandina
Evergreen shrub
Hardy to 0°F/–18°C
Part to full shade/moderate to regular water

The word "feathery" captures the essence of nandina. Unbranched, bamboolike stems rise from the ground to as high as 6 to 8 feet. Extending almost at right angles from the stems are large leaves consisting of countless lance-shaped leaflets that look like individual leaves.

New growth is pink tinted, reddish, or strongly bronzed, passing through a lettuce green stage before it matures to dark green. Chilling autumn weather gives leaves a reddish cast, and throughout winter the entire plant may be bright red. In mid- to late spring, airy pyramidal clusters of tiny white flowers appear at stem ends. When another plant is nearby for pollination, flowers are followed by large sprays of pea-size berries that ripen in autumn to brilliant red.

NANDINA domestica

Nurseries carry various named selections that vary in foliage width, plant height, and general shape. Among low-growing selections are 'Harbour Dwarf' (to 2 feet), 'Woods Dwarf' (to 4 feet), and 'Compacta' (to 5 feet). Two different foot-high plants are sold under the name 'Nana'. One has broad leaflets that look puffy and quilted; the other has narrow leaflets and spreads into colonies of stems, making a good ground cover.

Culture. Best and fastest growth comes in good soil with regular watering during dry periods. Established plants, though, are fairly drought tolerant and will grow in competition with tree roots. To increase bushiness and maintain foliage all the way down to the ground, you can cut back stems at various heights to force branching just below each cut.

Good companions. *Arbutus, Buxus, Camellia, Epimedium, Euonymus, Juniperus, Podocarpus.*

❧ OPHIOPOGON

See Liriope, page 93

❧ OSMANTHUS

Osmanthus
Evergreen shrubs
Hardy to 0°F/–18°C except as noted
Part shade/moderate to regular water

Glossy foliage on dense, orderly plants qualifies the *Osmanthus* species as serviceable basic shrubs. What sets them apart is their intoxicating floral fragrance. In most cases the flowers are inconspicuous, the aroma beckoning you from who-knows-where.

Sweet olive, *O. fragrans*, possesses the most penetrating fragrance—a fruity aroma (rather like apricots) that carries some distance. It comes from tiny white flowers that are most abundant in spring and summer but appear sporadically at other times. Unpruned, a plant can reach 10 or more feet high and wide, clothed in glossy oval leaves. Its orange-flowered form, *O. f. aurantiacus*, flowers principally in autumn on a more slender plant.

Holly-leaf osmanthus, *O. heterophyllus*, has spiny leaves that almost could pass for English holly. The scented blossoms of late autumn and winter form blue-black, berrylike fruits. Plants can reach 15 to 20 feet high and about half as wide. Among named selections are two especially dense growers that make good hedges, 'Gulftide' and 'Ilicifolius'. Slow-growing 'Rotundifolius' (to 5 feet) has

OSMANTHUS delavayi

small, nearly round leaves; 'Purpureus' features purple new growth and purplish leaves. 'Variegatus' has ivory-edged leaves on a 5-foot shrub, while the slightly shorter 'Goshiki' offers dark green leaves with yellow markings.

A hybrid of the two preceding species, *O. × fortunei* is a bit less hardy: to 5°F/–15°C. Leaves are spiny-margined and larger than the holly-leaf parent, on a slow-growing plant to 20 feet high. White flowers come in spring and summer, but the selection 'San Jose' has cream to orange blossoms in autumn.

The one species with something of a floral show is Delavay osmanthus, *O. delavayi*, hardy to 5°F/–15°C. Its arching branches form a mounding-spreading plant to 6 feet high and wider, with inch-long glossy leaves. Clusters of tubular white flowers appear by midspring.

Culture. None of the *Osmanthus* species is fussy about soil, and established plants will accept little to moderate watering.

Good companions. *Acanthus, Acer, Aucuba, Camellia, Hydrangea, Rhaphiolepis.*

❧ PACHYSANDRA *terminalis*

Japanese spurge
Evergreen subshrub
Hardy to –20°F/–29°C
Part shade/regular water

Handsome leaves and the ability to thrive in deep shade—even among shallow-rooted trees—have made Japanese spurge a top choice among evergreen ground covers. Oval leaves to 4 inches long are carried in whorls toward the ends of upright stems, forming an even, lustrous green carpet about 10 inches high when grown in shade or 6 inches high in partial shade.

Plants spread at a moderate rate by underground runners, sending up more and more stems as they increase their territory. In late spring, spikes of small, fluffy white flowers appear at stem tips; small white fruits may follow.

'Silveredge' and 'Variegata' offer variegated foliage—especially attractive in fully shaded locations. 'Green Carpet' is lower-growing (to about 4 inches in shade) and more compact.

PACHYSANDRA terminalis

Culture. For best appearance, plant Japanese spurge in reasonably good, slightly acid soil amended with organic matter. Keep watered during dry periods.

Good companions. *Acer, Camellia, Cornus, Enkianthus, Halesia, Rhododendron, Taxus.*

❧
PARTHENOCISSUS

Woodbine
Deciduous vines
Hardiness varies
Part to full shade/regular water

Glorious autumn foliage color is the hallmark of these handsome vines; clusters of small blue-black fruits are a bonus. Great vigor and potential size characterize the two most familiar species.

PARTHENOCISSUS tricuspidata

Boston ivy, *P. tricuspidata,* is the "ivy" that gave its name to the collegiate Ivy League. Hardy to –30°F/–34°C, plants cling tenaciously to wood, brick, or stone surfaces to create a solid foliage cover. Broad, 3-lobed glossy leaves somewhat like grape foliage can reach 8 inches across. 'Veitchii' and 'Lowii' are smaller-leafed selections; 'Beverly Brooks' has larger foliage and red autumn color, while 'Green Showers' has bigger leaves that turn a rich burgundy shade.

Native Virginia creeper, *P. quinquefolia,* is hardy to –35°F/–37°C. Its 6-inch leaves are divided into 5 distinct leaflets, producing a more open foliage cover than Boston ivy on an equally vigorous but more meandering vine. 'Engelmannii' is a denser, smaller-leafed selection.

Less well known is silvervein creeper, *P. henryana,* hardy to 0°F/–18°C. Foliage resembles Virginia creeper at half the size; purplish new growth matures to dark bronzy green with silver veins on top, burgundy red underneath. Leaves turn bright red in autumn. This is a relatively small vine, to about 20 feet.

Culture. These are woodland vines by nature and therefore grow well in "woodsy" soil: organically enriched and fairly well-drained. But they are not at all particular, accepting soils from light to heavy. Give them regular watering at first; established plants usually can get by with just moderate watering thereafter.

Good companions. *Aucuba, Buxus, Cornus, Hydrangea, Ilex, Juniperus, Taxus.*

❧
PIERIS

Pieris
Evergreen shrubs
Hardiness varies
Part shade/regular water

At all times of the year, these are neat, refined, elegant shrubs. The handsome leaves alone make them worth planting: lance-shaped, leathery, and glossy, often starting out bright pink, red, or bronze. Lavish floral displays consist of urn-shaped little flowers clustered (usually) like bunches of grapes at branch ends. Most plants form buds by autumn, so flower clusters are subtly decorative throughout winter.

Three species are common in the nursery trade. The hardiest is mountain pieris, *P. floribunda (Andromeda floribunda),* taking temperatures to –20°F/–29°C. Upright clusters of white flowers distinguish this species, a 6-foot shrub rounded to spreading in shape.

Next hardiest, to –10°F/–23°/C, is *P. japonica (Andromeda japonica),* called lily-of-the-valley shrub for reasons its white, pink, or red blossoms make obvious. Ultimately a 10-foot-high shrub, it carries its branches in tiers or layers. Among named selections, 'Variegata' has ivory-variegated leaves, while leaves of 'Bert Chandler' go through an orange-pink-cream-white color progression before maturing to light green. 'Mountain Fire' has particularly vivid red new growth. 'Flamingo' and 'Valley Valentine' both have rose-red

PIERIS 'Forest Flame'

flowers; 'Christmas Cheer' blooms red and white.

Chinese pieris, *P. forrestii,* is hardy to 0°F/–18°C. Its new growth is pink to red on a broad shrub ultimately reaching 10 feet tall; flowers are white. Its hybrid 'Forest Flame' has all-red new growth.

Culture. These rhododendron relatives thrive under rhododendron conditions: high shade or dappled sunlight; well-drained but moisture-retentive, acid soil; and a climate that is cool to warm in summer and not dry.

Good companions. *Acer, Alchemilla, Asarum, Cornus, Epimedium, Hosta, Rhododendron.*

PITTOSPORUM tobira 'Variegata'

❧
PITTOSPORUM

Pittosporum
Evergreen trees and shrubs
Hardiness varies
Part shade/moderate to regular water

Three pittosporum species are dependable basic landscape shrubs in the Pacific Coast states. One of them, *P. tobira,* is also at home in the lower South. All feature glossy, elliptical leaves; dense and orderly growth; and clusters of fragrant small flowers in spring.

West Coast gardeners who live where temperatures stay above 15°F/–9°C know *P. eugenioides* and *P. tenuifolium* as first-rate hedge, screen, and background shrubs. Their growth is upright, dense, and quite slender—easily kept that way with periodic clipping plus heading back

PLATYCODON grandiflorus

to maintain a given height. Left to their own devices, isolated plants can become trees 40 feet tall and half as wide.

Texture is the chief difference between the two species. Wavy-edged leaves, yellow-green to medium green in color, reach 4 inches long on *P. eugenioides;* a form with cream leaf margins stays shrubby to about 10 feet. *Pittosporum tenuifolium* has darker, broader, smoother-edged leaves 1½ inches long; selected forms offer variegated and bronze-purple leaves. Flowers are yellow on *P. eugenioides,* dark purple on *P. tenuifolium.*

Tobira, *P. tobira,* makes a dense, rounded, sometimes billowy shrub to around 15 feet high. Plants are hardy to –5°F/–21°C. Old specimens can become tree height, easily converted into multi-trunked trees by removing lower limbs. Glossy, dark green 5-inch leaves radiate around stems and group in whorls toward branch tips—an effective setting for springtime clusters of white flowers scented like orange blossoms. Fruits the size of garbanzo beans mature to tannish orange in autumn, then split open to reveal sticky orange seeds.

The lower-growing 'Variegata' has gray-green leaves edged white. 'Wheeler's Dwarf' is a 2-foot-high version of the species; 'Cream de Mint' is its counterpart with gray-green, white-edged leaves. 'Turner's Variegated Dwarf' changes the variegation to cream color.

Culture. None of the pittosporums is particular about soil. Plants look best when they receive routine watering, but established plants will endure dry periods.

Good companions. *Acanthus, Buxus, Hedera, Juniperus, Trachelospermum.*

❧
PLATYCODON grandiflorus

Balloon flower
Deciduous perennial
Hardy to –35°F/–37°C
Part shade/regular water

Nearly spherical, balloonlike buds give this plant its common name; the open blossoms resemble wide-open *Campanula* bells. Flowers appear toward the ends of upright, 2½- to 3-foot stems clothed in broadly oval, 3-inch leaves. Lavender-blue is the usual color, but there are variants with pink, white, and double flowers—as well as a foot-high dwarf. The bushy plants start flowering in early summer and can continue for 2 months or more if you remove spent blossoms.

Culture. The best soil for balloon flower is rather light, well-drained, and amended with organic matter. Locate plants in light shade or filtered sunlight.

Good companions. *Astilbe, Campanula, Corydalis, Francoa, Hosta, Lamium, Lilium, Liriope.*

❧
PODOCARPUS

Podocarpus
Evergreen trees and shrubs
Hardiness varies
Part shade/regular water

Although the word "pine" appears in the common names of podocarpus species, these trees and shrubs eventually produce fleshy fruits rather than true cones. Plants are either male or female, and a male plant must be nearby in order for a female plant to form fruits. Both species described here are slender plants with clean-looking, narrow leaves. Their slow growth keeps them shrubby for many years, but in time they develop into definite trees with 60-foot potential.

PODOCARPUS gracilior

Fern pine, *P. gracilior* (newly classified as *Afrocarpus gracilior,* also sold as *P. elongatus*), is hardy to 20°F/–7°C. Its growth habit depends on how the plant was propagated. Seed-grown plants are fairly upright, with narrow, 2- to 4-inch dark green leaves rather sparsely set on the branches. After a number of years, plants produce shorter, grayish to bluish green leaves spaced more closely together on branches.

Plants grown from cuttings or grafts of an older tree have the shorter, grayer, denser leaves as youngsters—on limber branches with little inclination toward strong vertical growth. These plants usually are sold as *P. elongatus;* the larger-leafed, more upright kinds are typically labeled *P. gracilior.* Both need staking until strong upright trunks develop; even so, older elongatus-type plants will exhibit drooping branches.

Hardier yew pine, *P. macrophyllus,* will take temperatures down to 0°F/–18°C. Leaves are bright green and narrow, to 4 inches long. This is a stiffer-looking, more decidedly upright plant than fern pine, with fairly horizontal

POLEMONIUM caeruleum

branching and slightly drooping branchlets. Shrubby yew pine, *P. m. maki,* is a dense, upright, slow-growing shrub clothed in very narrow 3-inch leaves.

Culture. Yew and fern pines grow well in most soils, though leaves may become yellow from chlorosis in soil that is alkaline or heavy and damp.

Good companions. *Aucuba, Buxus, Camellia, Euonymus, Ilex, Juniperus, Rhaphiolepis.*

POLEMONIUM caeruleum

Jacob's ladder
Deciduous perennial
Hardy to –40°F/–40°C
Part to full shade/regular water

The "ladder" in this plant's common name derives from the narrow leaflets that "climb" the central leafstalk, decreasing in length toward the top. Rosette-like clumps of the ferny foliage send up 1½- to 2-foot leafy stems in late spring to early summer, each crowned with a loose cluster of nodding, bell-shaped blue blossoms. With some searching at nurseries, you may find a white-flowered form.

Culture. Given average to good soil and routine watering, Jacob's ladder will be a foliage and flower asset in the foreground of a woodland garden planting.

Good companions. *Campanula, Dicentra, ferns, Helleborus, Hosta, Lilium, Platycodon.*

POLYGONATUM

Solomon's seal
Deciduous perennials
Hardy to –30°F/–34°C
Part to full shade/regular water

Grace and refinement mark the Solomon's seals. Gradually spreading clumps consist of slightly arching stems bearing pairs of broadly oval leaves arranged almost horizontally. Where

leaves join stems, pairs or clusters of small, bell-shaped white flowers hang on threadlike stalks. After flowering, small blue-black berries may form.

Tallest of the group is *P. commutatum* (sometimes sold as *P. canaliculatum* and now considered a form of *P. biflorum*); it can grow 4 to 5 feet high, bearing 7-inch leaves. Small Solomon's seal, *P. biflorum,* reaches about 3 feet, while the cream-margined leaves of *P. odoratum* 'Variegatum' come on stems in the 2- to 3-foot range. For an ankle-height clump or small ground cover, look for dwarf Japanese Solomon's seal, *P. falcatum.*

POLYGONATUM odoratum 'Variegatum'

Culture. Solomon's seals will tolerate less-than-regular watering and competition from tree roots. But their best performance comes in organically-rich soil that is always moist but not saturated.

Good companions. *Alchemilla, Astilbe, Bergenia, Epimedium, Helleborus, Hosta.*

PRIMULA

Primrose
Deciduous and evergreen perennials
Hardy to –20°F/–29°C except as noted
Part shade/regular to frequent water

The word "primrose" evokes images of woodlands and wildflowers, the essence of spring charm. In truth, these are plants for woodland conditions, and there is a vast assortment of species, hybrids, and hybrid strains from which to choose.

Specialists have organized primroses into 34 sections of species that resemble each other and usually need the same conditions. Only a handful of the sections, though, include plants that are easy for the average gardener to grow, and these can be divided into two general categories: those that prosper under ordinary garden conditions, and those that need abundant moisture—even to the point of growing in boggy soil.

All primrose plants form rosettes of leaves, above which the flowers are borne in three possible fashions: on individual stems, clustered at ends of stems, or in clusters going up the stems in tiers. Blossoms are circular in outline but composed of five lobes, each indented at its apex—in some types so deeply that the flower appears to have 10 parts. The earliest-blooming types begin in mid- to late winter in mild climates, but most flower sometime in spring. A very few have early summer blossoms.

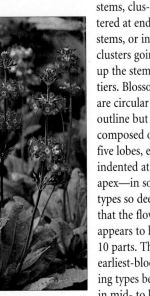

PRIMULA,
Candelabra type

• *Primroses for ordinary garden conditions.* The mass-marketed polyanthus hybrid primroses, P. × *polyantha,* are the most adaptable of all. In midwinter to early spring, their 6- to 12-inch stems bear clusters of yellow-centered flowers in white, cream, yellow, orange, red, pink, purple, blue, or bronzed tones. Tongue-shaped, textured 8-inch leaves look like romaine lettuce.

English primrose, *P. vulgaris,* resembles a smaller version of the polyanthus types; fragrant early-spring flowers are yellow in the species, variously colored in hybrids, which include the fine Barnhaven, Biedermeier, and Nosegay strains. Juliana primroses—hybrids of *P. juliae*—

are shorter, smaller, broader-leaved editions of polyanthus primroses, blooming in the same season in nearly as broad a range of colors.

Aptly referred to as "drumstick primrose," early spring–blooming *P. denticulata* presents its ½-inch pink, lavender, or white flowers in ball-shaped clusters atop foot-high stems over polyanthus-like foliage. Plants are hardy to –30°F/–34°C and will also grow in nearly as much dampness as the moisture-preferring types described below.

Several points mark *P. sieboldii* as different. Arrow-shaped leaves come at the ends of slender leafstalks; phloxlike flowers are clustered on 4- to 8-inch stems in late spring (white, lilac, pink, purple), and foliage dies down soon after plants finish flowering.

• *Primroses for damp soil.* Soil that's organically rich but moist or poorly drained suits quite a few primroses. Prominent among these are members of two of the 34 primrose sections: Candelabra (Proliferae) and Sikkimensis.

Candelabra primroses make large plants, some forming clumps 2½ feet across and raising stems 3 feet high. Flowers come in tiered whorls; the lowest tier opens first, just above the leaves, and then successive whorls come into bloom as the stem elongates. Five species, along with some selections and hybrids, are notable. These include *P. japonica* (purple, red, pink, white), *P. beesiana* (red-purple), *P.* × *bullesiana* (pink, cream, lavender), *P. pulverulenta* (red to magenta), and yellow-flowered *P. bulleyana* and *P. helodoxa.*

Sikkimensis primroses offer their fragrant bell-shaped blossoms in early summer, clustered atop sturdy but gracefully nodding stems. *P. sikkimensis* displays yellow flowers on 1½-foot stems. Three-foot stems, with as many as 60 flowers to a cluster, are characteristic of yellow *P. florindae*—which will grow in several inches of gently moving water. Hybrids offer orange and red blossoms, too.

Culture. Ideal primrose conditions, replicating native habitats, are organically rich soil and cool, moist atmosphere. The kinds that perform well under ordinary garden conditions need organically-amended soil as well as watering during any dry period. The damp-soil types will grow easily beside streams and ponds where soil is perpetually moist to soggy—but they'll take regular garden beds if you amend soil liberally with organic matter and go heavy on the watering.

All primroses are at home in the climates of the Pacific Northwest and Pacific coastal regions that are subject to fog and overcast. In warmer, drier regions, the primroses most likely to succeed are the rugged polyanthus types, Juliana hybrids, and summer-dormant *P. sieboldii.* Where winter chill is negligible or lacking, rely on the polyanthus hybrids.

Good companions. *Asarum, Bergenia, Dicentra, ferns, Hosta, Mertensia, Polygonatum, Pulmonaria.*

PRUNELLA

Self-heal
Evergreen perennials
Hardy to –20°F/–29°C
Part shade/regular water

The self-heals show a marked resemblance to their *Ajuga* relatives (see page 62), and like them they are useful as small-scale ground covers or "patch" plants along paths or at the foreground of lightly shaded beds. The plants make

PRUNELLA grandiflora

low, spreading clumps of 2- to 4-inch leaves; in summer, leafy flowering stems rise above the foliage, bearing elongated hooded flowers.

The largest of the readily available species is *P. grandiflora*. Its flowering stems can reach 1½ feet high, typically offering purple blossoms; there are also named selections with white, pink, and lilac flowers. Plants labeled *P. webbiana* resemble *P. grandiflora* but have shorter leaves; named selections include larger-flowered 'Loveliness' (lavender), 'Pink Loveliness', and 'White Loveliness'. Plant purple-flowered *P. vulgaris* with caution: it can spread and self-sow to the point of becoming a weed.

Culture. The self-heals are rugged, deep-rooted plants that look best when planted in average to good soil and given regular moisture. Plant them where they can spread without becoming a nuisance or overwhelming delicate plants.

Good companions. *Anemone, Aspidistra, Cercis, ferns, ornamental grasses, Nandina.*

❧
PULMONARIA

Lungwort
Deciduous and evergreen perennials
Hardy to –35°F/–37°C except as noted
Part to full shade/regular water

The lungworts offer attractive blossoms, but much of their charm derives from good-looking foliage. Hairy leaves, broadly oval to lance-shaped, form rosettes or clumps low to the ground; a number of species and named selections feature green leaves highlighted by silver or gray mottling. In late spring, flowering stems bear smaller leaves beneath nodding clusters of trumpet-shaped blossoms.

For beautifully silver-spotted leaves, evergreen Bethlehem sage, *P. saccharata*, is available in named selections that give you a choice of flower colors from white to blue to pink aging to blue. When in flower, plants reach 12 to 18 inches tall.

PULMONARIA longifolia 'Bertram Anderson'

Heavily spotted foliage also is a feature of *P. longifolia*, which differs in its long and narrow leaves, shorter flower stems bearing violet-blue blossoms, and deciduous habit. Jerusalem cowslip, *P. officinalis*, features mottled, heart-shaped deciduous leaves and reddish buds opening to lilac-blue flowers on a 1- to 1½-foot plant.

Solidly green, deciduous foliage is characteristic of two additional species. Foot-high blue lungwort, *P. angustifolia*, typically has dark green leaves and pink buds opening as bright blue blossoms. Greater height (to 2 feet) and light green foliage mark *P. rubra*, hardy only to –20°F/–29°C; its coral pink flowers appear in very early spring.

Culture. The lungworts need a well-drained, organically enriched soil that is always moist. Partial to full shade is a must: leaves can wilt temporarily in sunlight even when soil is moist.

Use lungworts in clumps, in drifts, or as small-scale ground covers in woodland gardens—along pathways, under deciduous trees and shrubs.

Good companions. *Dicentra, ferns, Hosta, Mertensia, Polygonatum, Primula, Trillium.*

RHAMNUS californica 'Eve Case'

❧
RHAMNUS

Buckthorn
Deciduous and evergreen shrubs
Hardiness varies
Part shade/moderate water

The buckthorns are no-problem, attractive foliage plants that are useful as hedges and as background for showier subjects. All have small, berrylike fruits.

Hardiest of the lot is deciduous alder buckthorn, *R. frangula*, to –40°F/–40°C. This dense plant matures at a height and spread of 10 to 18 feet, clothed in broadly oval, 2½-inch dark green leaves that turn yellow in autumn. Pea-size berries form over an extended period, changing from greenish yellow to orange-red to dark red to black. Tallhedge buckthorn, *R. f.* 'Columnaris', is a first-rate hedge plant, reaching 12 to 18 feet high (unless trimmed) but making a compact, vertical plant no more than about 4 feet wide.

Two evergreen species are hardy to 0°F/–18°C. Italian buckthorn, *R. alaternus*, makes a dense, billowy plant 12 to 20 feet high and wide with upward-sweeping branches. Its pea-size fruits are black, its 2-inch oval leaves bright green and glossy; the selection 'Variegata' ('Argenteovariegata') has leaves with broad ivory margins and irregular gray-green blotches.

Coffeeberry, *R. californica*, is a variably upright plant to 15 feet with 3-inch glossy, oval leaves. Two widely sold named selections are 'Eve Case', a compact, rounded shrub 4 to 8 feet high; and 'Seaview', which can spread to 8 feet but is easily kept under 2 feet high with slight pruning. Both have broadly oval leaves to 6 inches long; cherry-size fruits change from red to black as they mature.

Culture. You can plant buckthorns in good soil and give them routine watering—they'll grow very well. But they also thrive in nutrient- and organically-poor soil and with only moderate moisture during dry periods.

RHAPHIOLEPIS indica

Good companions. *Aucuba, Berberis, Hedera, Hypericum, Juniperus, Mahonia, Rhaphiolepis.*

❧
RHAPHIOLEPIS indica

Rhaphiolepis, India hawthorn
Evergreen shrub
Hardy to 10°F/–12°C
Part shade/moderate to regular water

Within its hardiness range, India hawthorn comes close to being a perfect shrub. Plants are rounded and symmetrical, growing densely with a full cover of leathery oval leaves. The ½-inch single flowers appear in dense, sizeable clusters over a 4- to 5-month period. Subtle color touches come with bronzy new leaves and blue-black berries that may form after flowers fade.

Nurseries offer quite a few named selections, differing in flower color and plant size. Among those growing 4 feet or taller are 'Clara' (white), 'Enchantress' (soft pink), 'Jack Evans' (bright pink), 'Pink Lady' (deep pink), 'Spring Rapture' (rosy red), 'Springtime' (deep pink), and 'White Enchantress'. In the 2- to 4-foot range are 'Ballerina' (deep pink), 'Charisma' (pink, with double flowers), 'Coates Crimson' (deepest pink), and 'Pink Cloud' (deep pink).

Culture. The widespread use of these shrubs in landscaping testifies to their ease of culture. All they need is average soil and, for best appearance, routine watering during dry periods.

Good companions. *Acanthus, Ajuga, Bergenia, Buxus, Juniperus, Nandina, Podocarpus.*

❧
RHODODENDRON

Rhododendron, azalea
Deciduous and evergreen shrubs
Hardiness varies
Part to full shade/regular water

A visit to a neighborhood nursery may only hint at the diversity that the genus *Rhododendron* encompasses. The International Register records more than 10,000 named selections and hybrids, of which perhaps 2,000 are sold today! Botanists recognize approximately 800 species of *Rhododendron*, arranged in series and subseries. One of these series includes the plants called azaleas.

With a group of plants this size, it's not easy to generalize. But this much can safely be said of rhododendrons and azaleas. They are valued for a dazzling color display which spans a possible 6-month period from midwinter through late spring. The basic flower is funnel shaped (though there are exceptions), and flowers appear in tightly knit clusters. Only true blue is missing from the color palette, though some come close. Most importantly, virtually all rhododendrons and azaleas share the same basic cultural needs. Visit nurseries and public gardens to see what is thriving in your area.

Based on standard nursery offerings, it's tempting to assert that azaleas are more fine-textured and lightweight-appearing, whereas rhododendrons are more massive and solid. Visit a specialist garden, however, and you'll find rhododendrons that range from ground-hugging creepers with flowers and leaves less

RHODODENDRON 'Anna Rose Whitney'

than an inch in size to treelike shrubs bearing volleyball-size flower clusters (called "trusses"). Foliage varies from glossy to matte, from veined and rough-looking to hairy to absolutely smooth. Hardiness varies considerably, too. Some of the old "ironclad" derivatives of *R. catawbiense* and the Dexter hybrids will take temperatures to –25°F/–32°C. A vast array of hybrids tolerate lows only in the range of 0°F/–18°C.

Azaleas are more nearly homogeneous, but you will find variation in plant, flower, and foliage sizes as well as both evergreen and deciduous plants. Evergreen azaleas are, for the most part, rounded plants that tend to be dense and twiggy; their flowers may be white, pink, red, purple, or lavender. There are numerous hybrid groups sharing similar appearance and hardiness, including Belgian Indicas (hardy to 20°F/–7°C); Gable hybrids (hardy to 0°F/–18°C); Glenn Dale hybrids (hardy to 0°F/–18°C); Kaempferi hybrids (hardy to –15°F/–26°C); Kurume hybrids (hardy to 5°F/–15°C); Rutherfordiana hybrids (hardy to 20°F/–7°C); Satsuki hybrids (hardy to 5°F/–15°C); and Southern Indicas (hardy to about 10°F/–12°C).

Deciduous azaleas offer flowers in bright yellow, orange, and flame red in addition to white, cream, and pink; plants tend to be more upright than spreading. Most widely sold are hybrid selections such as Exbury, Knap Hill, and Mollis. Hardiness varies—from about –40°F/–40°C for the Minnesota-bred Northern Lights hybrids to around –5°F/–21°C for Pacific Coast native *R. occidentale*. Most produce a show of autumn foliage color in yellow, orange, red, or maroon.

Culture. Climate can dictate success or failure with these plants. For rhododendrons, a cool, humid atmosphere is ideal, and for many cultivars it is essential. The best areas for rhododendrons include the Pacific Northwest (west of the Cascades) and the California coast down to about Monterey Bay; the Appalachian highlands, from northern Georgia into New

York; the Atlantic seaboard, from northern Delaware through New England; and areas west through New York, Pennsylvania, and parts of Ohio (especially near Lake Erie).

Azaleas can endure more heat and dryness, growing well in prime rhododendron territory as well as in much of California west of the Sierra Nevada plus the middle and deep South. Deciduous azaleas are the least demanding of all, tolerating dry heat (if well watered) and fairly ordinary garden soil.

Rhododendrons and azaleas make dense networks of fibrous roots that need both moisture and plenty of air in the soil. Therefore they need soil that is well drained but moist, and also cool and acid. Add copious amounts of organic matter to the soil before planting, and plant so that the tops of the root balls are several inches above soil grade. Keep a mulch over the soil at all times: pine needles, oak leaves, wood by-products, or even compost. Some growers who have poorly-draining clay soil actually set plants on top of amended existing soil, then cover roots and trunks nearly to the plants' bases with an extra-thick mulch.

Good companions. *Acer, Asarum, Camellia, Enkianthus, Epimedium, Halesia, Hosta, Pieris.*

❧

RIBES sanguineum

Pink winter currant,
red flowering currant
Deciduous shrub
Hardy to 0°F/–18°C
Part shade/moderate water

RIBES sanguineum

Gardeners in Pacific coastal states cherish pink winter currant for its overall charm and its good springtime flower display. Just before new leaves emerge, branches of this 4- to 12-foot shrub deck themselves out in grapelike hanging clusters of small pink blossoms. Blue-black fruits mature in summer, somewhat obscured by the hairy, 2½-inch lobed leaves resembling the foliage of some maples. Leaves turn rusty gold in autumn.

The usual plant offered in nurseries is *R. s. glutinosum*, with flowers that run from light to dark pink; choose plants in flower if you wish a specific color. Named selections offer an expanded color range including red ('Barrie Coate', 'Elk River Red', 'King Edward VII') and white ('Album', 'Inverness White', 'White Icicle'). Flowers of 'Claremont' are pink at first but age to red; 'Spring Showers' features 8-inch blossom clusters—twice the usual length.

Culture. Pink winter currant is not particular about soil. Water plants routinely during dry periods for their first year to get them established. Thereafter, they'll need just moderate watering where summer is warm to hot, little water in cool-summer areas. Plant habit depends somewhat on location: more compact and dense in plenty of light, more irregular and open as shade increases.

Good companions. *Arbutus, Berberis, Helleborus, Iris foetidissima, Juniperus, Mahonia, Rubus.*

❧

RUBUS pentalobus

Taiwan bramble
Evergreen ground cover shrub
Hardy to 0°F/–18°C
Part shade/moderate water

When you see this plant dotted with salmon-colored fruits, you'll recognize it as a blackberry. And the small, single white flowers that precede the edible fruits further the image. But this is not a brambly, prickly, thicket-forming shrub.

RUBUS pentalobus

Instead, thornless stems spread horizontally over the ground, building up a foliage mass around 1 foot high.

Leaves are generally round, to 1½ inches across, broadly lobed with ruffled margins; the dark green surface has a rough, crinkly appearance. Some leaves turn red or bronze in winter.

Nurseries usually offer this plant by one of its previous names, *R. calycinoides* or *R. fockeanus*. 'Emerald Carpet' is a superior selection.

Culture. Merely average, well-drained soil produces healthy growth. Plants will withstand dry periods, but foliage looks more lush with supplemental watering during dry spring and summer months.

Good companions. *Arbutus, Fatsia, Hypericum, Juniperus, Nandina, Rhaphiolepis, Ribes.*

❧

RUSCUS

Butcher's broom
Evergreen shrubs
Hardy to 0°F/–18°C
Part to full shade/moderate water

In addition to their attractive appearance and their ability to grow in deep shade, the butcher's brooms have curiosity

RUSCUS hypoglossum

SARCOCOCCA ruscifolia

value: they are leafless! What appear to be leaves are structures called cladodes—flattened stem tissue with a leafy appearance. Tiny, greenish white flowers appear in the centers of these leaflike structures. If both male and female plants are included in a planting (or if you have a plant that bears both male and female flowers), bright red marble-size fruits will be produced. Plants spread by underground stems, forming gradually expanding clumps.

Two species are generally available. The taller of the two, from 1 to 4 feet high, is *R. aculeatus*, with branching stems and spine-tipped, 3-inch cladodes of a dull, dark green. Its fruits may be red or yellow. Unbranched stems growing to 1½ feet high distinguish *R. hypoglossum*; its cladodes are glossy green, to 4 inches long, and spineless. Spreading at a moderate rate, it makes a good small-scale ground cover.

Culture. Butcher's brooms grow equally well in light or heavy soils. They'll tolerate dry soil, deep shade, even tree-root competition. But they also will perform well with reasonably good soil and routine garden watering.

Good companions. *Aucuba, Bergenia, Clivia, Fatsia, Ribes, Vancouveria.*

SARCOCOCCA

Sweet box, sarcococca
Evergreen shrubs
Hardy to 0°F/–18°C
Part to full shade/moderate to
regular water

You never would mistake this plant for the related boxwood (*Buxus,* page 70), but it does share the boxwood qualities of neatness and polish.

Low-growing *S. hookerana humilis* spreads at a fairly slow rate by underground runners to become a patch 8 or more feet across but just 1½ feet high. Leaves are pointed ovals to 3 inches long, very dark green and glossy. Hidden among the dense foliage in winter or early spring are tiny, highly fragrant white flowers that may be followed by blue-black fruits.

Sarcococca ruscifolia slowly grows into a spreading shrub 4 to 6 feet high clothed in 2-inch, glossy dark green leaves. Its tiny, scented blossoms are followed by red fruits. A similar species, *S. confusa*, often is sold as *S. ruscifolia*; it differs chiefly in that its fruits are black.

Culture. The sarcococcas grow best in a soil that has been liberally enriched with organic matter prior to planting. Given such soil, they'll prosper with regular to moderate watering, light to deep shade.

Good companions. *Aucuba, Azara, Camellia, Enkianthus, Hydrangea, Rhododendron.*

SKIMMIA

Skimmia
Evergreen shrubs
Hardy to 0°F/–18°C
Part shade/regular water

An air of good breeding surrounds the skimmias. Their growth is neat, orderly, and slow; their leaves are rich green and glossy; and clusters of small white flowers are held well above the foliage.

Hollylike red berries may appear as autumn and winter decoration.

An individual skimmia plant is a rounded mound of overlapping leaves. When a number of plants are massed—as along a pathway or for a small-scale ground cover—the foliage makes a virtually level surface.

A fragrance reminiscent of lily-of-the-valley emanates from the flowers of the most commonly sold species, *S. japonica*. In time this plant may grow 5 feet high and 6 feet across, stylishly outfitted in 3- to 4-inch oval leaves. Male

SKIMMIA japonica

and female flowers grow on separate plants; if both grow near enough for pollination to take place, female plants will bear fruits. An outstanding male plant is the selection 'Macrophylla', with larger leaves and flowers.

Another fragrant species is *S. reevesiana* (*S. fortunei*), which differs in two respects: its growth is lower (about 2 feet high and 3 feet wide), and the flowers are self-fertile, which assures a crop of dull red berries.

A presumed hybrid between these two species, *S. foremanii* can be characterized as a more compact version of *S. japonica* with broader foliage; some plants appear to be self-fertile.

Culture. The skimmias thrive in an acid soil with a liberal amendment of organic matter. Given the same climate and soil conditions that rhododendrons prefer (see page 102), these plants are easy to grow. In warmer, drier regions, *S. foremanii* is the most likely to succeed.

Good companions. *Enkianthus, Epimedium, Franklinia, Hamamelis, Nandina, Rhododendron.*

꙳

SOLEIROLIA soleirolii

Baby's tears, angel's tears
Evergreen perennial ground cover
Hardy to 10°F/–12°C
Full shade/regular water

Its appealing common names and delicate appearance mask this plant's tough and aggressive nature. Threadlike, interlacing stems bear countless tiny, emerald green leaves to create an undulating carpet that looks (and is) both cool and soft. In light or partial shade, this refreshing pool of green will remain close to the soil, but in full shade it can rise up to about 4 inches thick.

Wherever shade and regular moisture encourage it, baby's tears spreads quickly—an inexorable green tide that can become an invasive pest because the smallest pieces of stems will take root wherever they touch soil. Foot traffic easily injures the fleshy leaves and stems, spoiling the appearance, but rapid regrowth soon repairs such damage. In hard frosts, the lush green carpet becomes black mush; but at the onset of warm weather, new growth reappears from the roots.

SOLEIROLIA soleirolii

STEWARTIA koreana

With a bit of searching, you might find two foliage variants: 'Aurea' (golden green leaves) and 'Variegata' (white-variegated foliage).

Culture. Moisture and shade are the only requirements for success. Baby's tears will grow in virtually any type of soil, from sand to clay. In organically amended soils, growth may be more lush and rapid.

Good companions. *Camellia, Carex (see "Ornamental Grasses," page 78), Clivia, ferns, Liriope.*

꙳

STEWARTIA

Stewartia
Deciduous trees
Hardy to –10°F/–23°C
Part shade/regular water

These camellia relatives are refined trees that offer camellia-like single flowers in summer and outstanding foliage color in autumn. After leaves have fallen, you have a wintertime clear view of handsome, multicolored bark.

Japanese stewartia, *S. pseudocamellia*, is a narrowly pyramidal tree that may grow 30 or 40 feet tall after many years. Single white, somewhat cup-shaped flowers reach 2½ inches across; oval leaves turn bronze to purple in autumn. Botanists don't agree on whether Korean stewartia is a separate species, *S. koreana*, or merely a geographic variant of the

Japanese species. It has slightly larger leaves that color orange to red-orange in autumn, and 3-inch flowers that open more widely.

Tall stewartia, *S. monadelpha*, actually is the shortest of the three, growing to around 25 feet high. Its white flowers are a bit less than 2 inches across; in autumn, its narrow leaves become brilliant red before dropping.

Culture. The stewartias grow well under camellia conditions. Give them good, organically enriched, neutral to acid soil and a sheltered location with dappled sunlight to light or partial shade. They are good choices for the margin of a woodland planting—especially handsome against a backdrop of taller, darker-leafed trees. Success is limited to the Pacific Coast and mid-Atlantic states.

Good companions. *Camellia, Enkianthus, Hamamelis, Ilex, Leucothoe, Pieris, Rhododendron.*

TAXUS × media

꙳

TAXUS

Yew
Evergreen shrubs
Hardiness varies
Part to full shade/moderate to regular water

Dark, dense, and formal, yews are classic topiary plants appearing in fanciful shapes from pyramids and spheres to clipped animals. When not subjected to such rigid training, they make excellent hedge plants, screens, even individual specimens. All yews, in their basic form, will become treelike in time. Most widely planted, however, are variant forms that are definitely shrubby, spreading, or even slimly upright.

All yews have short, flattened, dark green needles that clothe the branches densely. Female trees bear cup-shaped fruits, usually bright scarlet; their seeds (as well as yew foliage) are poisonous if ingested.

English yew, *T. baccata*, is hardy to –10°F/–23°C. This species is best known through various selections that include two upright forms: 'Stricta', the Irish yew, which makes a broad, flat-topped column; and 'Erecta', more narrowly upright. Widely planted 'Repandens' has nearly horizontal branches that spread to 6 feet but rise only about 2 feet high. Notably short-needled 'Adpressa' is a dense, spreading shrub reaching about 5 feet high.

Japanese yew, *T. cuspidata*, is hardy to –20°F/–29°C. Its selection 'Capitata' grows as a dense pyramid eventually reaching 25 feet high if not restricted. Lower-growing forms, to around 4 feet, are 'Nana' and 'Densiformis'. Hybrids between Japanese and English yews are designated *T. × media* and are hardy to –20°F/–29°C. Named selections include 'Hicksii' and 'Hatfieldii', both about 20 feet, and 'Brownii', which reaches 8 feet as a broadly rounded cone.

Culture. Yews will grow in a variety of well-drained soils as long as they are neither strongly acid nor alkaline. These plants accept routine garden watering, but established yews will survive on just occasional watering, especially in cool-summer climates. In subfreezing winter climates, make sure plants will be sheltered from drying winter winds and bright sunlight.

Good companions. *Cornus, Fothergilla, Hamamelis, Hydrangea, Parthenocissus.*

🌿
THALICTRUM

Meadow rue
Deciduous perennials
Hardy to –20°F/–29°C
Part shade/regular water

Delicate and filmy, the meadow rues share two characteristics with the related columbines (*Aquilegia*, page 63): foliage that is fernlike and frequently blue-green, and preference for woodland-edge conditions. However, plant size and flower shape set them apart. The flowering stems of meadow rues rise 2 to 5 feet high, depending on the species, while the branched flower clusters carry numerous fluffy-looking little blossoms.

Two species raise their flowers to the 5-foot level. Lemon yellow is the blossom color of *T. speciosissimum*; the similar *T. rochebrunianum* and its selection 'Lavender Mist' introduce a cool note of lilac blue. Plants sold as *T. dipterocarpum* and *T. delavayi* represent just one species, though there is disagreement about which name is correct. Stems reach 4 to 5 feet high, displaying a haze of deep lilac to violet blossoms. In the selection 'Hewitt's Double', flowers appear more substantial because the stamens have been converted to petal-like segments.

At the short end of the scale is *T. aquilegifolium*, which has rosy lilac flow-

THALICTRUM aquilegifolium

ers that appear to be solely puffs of fluffy stamens.

Culture. Good soil, well amended with organic matter, will please the meadow rues. Plant them in light shade or dappled sunlight, and see that soil always is moist.

Good companions. *Aconitum, Alchemilla, Bergenia, Digitalis, ferns, Helleborus, Hosta.*

TIARELLA cordifolia

🌿
TIARELLA

Tiarella, false miterwort
Deciduous to evergreen perennials
Hardiness varies
Full shade/regular water

For subtle beauty and delicacy, the tiarellas take a front seat. Foliage clumps consist of long-stalked leaves that are lobed and maplelike or divided into three leaflets. In late spring or summer, threadlike stems rise a foot tall to present elongated, open clusters of tiny white or palest pink blossoms that seem to float in the air above the leaves.

The hardiest species—to –40°F/–40°C—are *T. cordifolia* and *T. wherryi*. In appearance they are quite similar, but one difference is important: *T. cordifolia*,

TRANDESCANTIA × *andersoniana*

commonly called foamflower, can spread rapidly by rhizomes and creeping stems called stolons; *T. wherryi* forms gradually-spreading clumps. The light green leaves of *T. cordifolia* may turn yellow and red in autumn.

Western foamflower or sugar-scoop, *T. trifoliata unifoliata*, features dark green leaves more deeply lobed than the other two species. It is hardy to about –20°F/–29°C and is adapted chiefly to its native Pacific Coast territory.

Culture. As woodland natives, the tiarellas need a woodland-type soil: well-drained and containing plenty of organic matter. Give them supplemental watering during dry periods.

Good companions. *Aconitum, Bletilla, Campanula, Lilium, Platycodon, Tricyrtis.*

TRACHELOSPERMUM jasminoides

TRACHELOSPERMUM
jasminoides

Star jasmine, Confederate jasmine
Evergreen vine
Hardy to 15°F/–9°C
Part shade/regular water

Versatility is one of star jasmine's selling points. Given support to twine on, it can climb 20 feet on a wall; or you can encourage it to wrap around a post. If you let it grow unsupported, it will spread out to become a solid ground cover, building to about a 2-foot depth. And if you grow it in a raised bed or at the top of a retaining wall, its stems will gracefully spill over the sides.

Star jasmine's handsome, 3-inch oval foliage is glossy dark green. From late spring into summer, plants are covered in clusters of inch-wide, pinwheel-shaped white blossoms that send an intense fragrance through the air.

Culture. Plant star jasmine in well-drained soil; for the most lush growth, fertilize as growth begins and again after flowers fade. In alkaline soil, plants may need treatment for the yellowed leaves that indicate chlorosis.

Good companions. *Acanthus, Azara, Buxus, Fatsia, Nandina, Pittosporum.*

TRADESCANTIA × andersoniana

Spiderwort
Deciduous perennial
Hardy to –20°F/–29°C
Part shade/regular water

When it's not flowering, a spiderwort clump might pass for some sort of grass. Each stem looks like a small corn plant, producing arching, straplike leaves on either side. By flowering time, a clump may reach 2 feet high, holding clusters of flower buds atop the stems. Each 1½-inch flower contains 3 broad petals that form a triangular outline; one day is a blossom's life span, but a seemingly inexhaustable supply of buds gives a long period of bloom.

Nurseries offer named selections (often under the species name *T. virginiana*) with flowers in purple, blue, pink, lilac, and white.

Culture. Spiderworts revel in organically enriched soil with plenty of water, but the soil itself can be anything from sand to clay. In truth, the plants are virtually abuse-proof—though at a sacrifice to appearance.

As summer progresses, clumps can become leggy and sprawling. At that point you can cut plants back nearly to the ground; they'll come back with new growth almost immediately, sometimes giving a second show of flowers before going dormant in autumn.

Good companions. *Alchemilla, Brunnera, Digitalis, Filipendula, Myosotis, Trollius.*

TRICYRTIS

Toad lily
Deciduous perennials
Hardy to 0°F/–18°C
Part to full shade/regular water

The word "orchidlike" captures the unusual beauty of toad lily blossoms. Each flower contains three petals and three sepals, arranged in starlike fashion; rising from the center is a column of decorative stamens and styles. Usually a light background color is liberally spot-

TRICYRTIS 'Miyazaki'

ted in a shade of purple. Upright to arching stems are clasped by broadly oval leaves; flowers appear in clusters at stem ends and at leaf bases during summer and into autumn.

The most common species, *T. hirta*, also is one of the tallest, with arching stems growing to 3 feet; purple-spotted flowers are white or pale lilac, but all-white selections are also available. Another 3-footer, *T.* 'Miyazaki', has arching stems, narrower leaves, and lilac-dotted white flowers. Upright stems to 2½ feet characterize *T. formosana*, which bears most flowers at stem ends; lilac-spotted white is typical, but 'Amethystina' has lavender flowers with dark red markings.

Culture. Toad lilies are woodland plants that appreciate organically enriched, well-drained but moist soil. In time, *T. formosana* will spread by underground stems into broad patches; the other toad lilies will remain in more discrete clumps. Volunteer seedlings often are a ready source of additional plants.

Good companions. *Asarum, Bergenia, Helleborus, Hosta, Liriope, Pulmonaria, Trillium.*

TRILLIUM

Trillium, wake robin
Deciduous perennials
Hardiness varies
Part shade/regular water

Growing in the dappled sunlight beneath bare and newly leafed-out branches, elegant trilliums are a favorite harbinger of spring . The "tri" part of the name derives from the fact that all plant parts appear in groups of three: a whorl of three leaves tops a short stem, and nested in the whorl is a three-petaled flower backed by three green sepals. When in flower, most species reach 1 to 1½ feet high; plants die down by mid- to late summer.

Many species are found in eastern and western North America and are

TRILLIUM grandiflorum

well-adapted within their native areas; native plant specialists often offer them. Several species are more generally available, including eastern native *T. grandiflorum*, which bears 3-inch white flowers that age to pink. Plants are hardy to –40°F/–40°C. The selection 'Roseum' had pink flowers, while 'Flore Pleno' is a double white form that resembles a gardenia. Another eastern native, hardy to –30°F/–34°C. is *T. sessile*, which has mottled leaves as a backdrop to upright-petaled, maroon blossoms.

Western native species come close to duplicating their eastern kin. Narrower white petals are the most obvious distinction of *T. ovatum (T. californicum)*, which otherwise resembles *T. grandiflorum*. It is hardy to –20°F/–29°C. Similar to *T. sessile* is *T. chloropetalum*, which has the mottled leaves and upright flower petals in yellow to maroon; plants take temperatures down to –10°F/–23°C.

Culture. All trilliums need a deep and well-drained soil, well enriched with organic matter. Plants need regular moisture from the moment they start growing until they die down. During their dormant months, see that the ground is watered periodically so that the deep roots never become totally dry.

Good companions. *Asarum, Doronicum, Hosta, Mertensia, Polygonatum, Primula, Pulmonaria.*

TROLLIUS

Globeflower
Deciduous perennials
Hardy to –30°F/–34°C
Part shade/regular to frequent water

These are not plants for the water-rationed garden. But if you can give them the abundant moisture they crave, you'll be rewarded by brilliant blossoms carried above lush mounds of handsome foliage. Leaves are rather finely cut, almost celerylike in appearance. Yellow to orange flowers, often cup- or globe-shaped, grow at the end of 2- to 3-foot-tall stems rising from the foliage clumps. Some globeflowers blossom in spring, some in summer; all will flower longer if you remove spent blossoms.

Trollius europaeus 'Superbus' offers butter yellow, globular flowers on 2-foot stems in mid-spring. Late spring into summer is the flowering period of the hybrids listed under *T.* × *cultorum*—including 'Lemon Queen' (2 feet), 'Golden Monarch (2½ feet), and orange-flowered 'Etna' (3 feet).

TROLLIUS chinensis 'Golden Queen'

Plants listed as *T. ledebourii* are more likely *T. chinensis*, with flowers consisting of broad, cupped outer petals and a central cluster of narrow, upright ones. Widely sold is summer-flowering *T. c.* 'Golden Queen', with yellow-orange flowers on 2- to 3-foot stems.

Culture. Really moist soil is the key to globeflower success. In ordinary garden beds, liberally amend soil with organic matter, then water regularly. The continually damp ground alongside a pond or stream will be to these plants' liking.

Good companions. *Aruncus, Astilbe, Cimicifuga, Filipendula, Hosta, Ligularia.*

TSUGA

Hemlock
Evergreen trees and shrubs
Hardiness varies
Part shade/regular water

The ultimate size of hemlocks—40 feet or greater—generally puts them in the role of shade-casters rather than shade-dwellers. However, under certain circumstances two species can fit into the partially shaded garden.

Hemlocks are conifers, in a league with junipers, pines, and the like, but they possess a grace and softness that sets them apart. Their foliage consists of flattened needles less than an inch long; plants are dense and compact, with slightly pendulous branches.

Canada or Eastern hemlock, *T. canadensis*, is hardy to –30°F/–34°C; Carolina hemlock, *T. caroliniana*, takes temperatures to –20°F/–29°C. These are similar plants, equally graceful, that can be maintained as rather formal but soft-appearing hedges with just an annual trimming. Canada hemlock is the choice

TSUGA canadensis 'Pendula'

for cooler climates and clear air; Carolina hemlock is the better candidate in urban areas with their attendant air pollution.

Canada hemlock has produced a number of dwarf variants, the best known of which is *T. c.* 'Pendula', the Sargent weeping hemlock. This grows as a low, spreading mound to perhaps 4 feet high and 8 feet wide, giving the effect of a particularly elegant juniper.

Culture. Hemlocks need atmospheric moisture and summer rainfall, limiting their usefulness to eastern North America, the Pacific Northwest, and the Northern California coastal region. Give them regular moisture, acid soil, and shelter from strong wind.

Good companions. *Acer, Cercidiphyllum, Cercis, Cornus, Franklinia, Stewartia.*

VANCOUVERIA

Vancouveria
Deciduous and evergreen perennials
Hardy to 0°F/–18°C
Part shade/moderate to regular water

Closely related to *Epimedium* as well as to the shrubby *Berberis* and *Mahonia* species, the vancouverias nevertheless look more like overgrown maidenhair fern. Wirelike leafstalks grow directly from underground stems, bearing numerous broad leaflets that resemble small ivy leaves. Little yellow or white flowers (depending on the species) appear on threadlike stalks above the foliage in late spring or early summer. Plants spread into large clumps or patches, making the vancouverias fine ground covers and pathway plants for light shade or dappled sunlight.

Deciduous *V. hexandra* has light green leaves that make a foliage mass 4 to 16 inches high; white blossoms come in few-flowered clusters. Evergreen *V. planipetala*, called inside-out flower and sometimes sold as *V. parviflora*, makes a carpet of foliage that can rise to 2 feet.

VANCOUVERIA planipetala

Tiny white flowers with backward-swept segments come in airy clusters of up to 50 blossoms. Yellow flowers, as many as 15 on each stem, distinguish *V. chrysantha*; its bronzed gray-green foliage mass can grow 16 inches high.

Culture. Vancouverias appreciate an organically amended, woodland type of soil, but they are not demanding plants. Give them regular watering to establish them. In years following, they will thrive with merely occasional summer watering in cool-summer regions, moderate to regular watering during dry periods where summer is warm to hot and dry.

Good companions. *Acer, Bergenia, Camellia, Dicentra, ferns, Helleborus, Rhododendron.*

VIBURNUM

Viburnum
Deciduous and evergreen shrubs
Hardiness varies
Part shade/regular water

The many viburnum species and hybrids include some of the best medium-size to large shrubs for general landscaping purposes. Most have clustered flowers in white or pink that make a winter or spring show, often followed by decorative, berrylike fruits in red, blue, or black. Many of the deciduous sorts give a good display of autumn foliage in red or purplish red.

Nearly all viburnums will take a bit of shade—as in a location where they get morning sun but become shaded at some

VIBURNUM tinus

point in the afternoon as trees intercept the sun. The following four species, though, are well-adapted to light shade or dappled sunlight throughout the day.

Deciduous nannyberry, *V. lentago*, is the hardiest of the quartet, taking temperatures as low as –50°F/–46°C. Its glossy oval leaves (purplish red in autumn) clothe a truly bulky shrub that can reach well over 20 feet in height and spread—or can be trained as a tree to about 30 feet tall. Its white spring flowers come in flat clusters, later forming bird-alluring fruits that are red at first, becoming black at maturity.

Chinese snowball, *V. macrocephalum macrocephalum*, is hardy to –10°F/–23°C. Deciduous in colder climates (without colorful autumn foliage), it's nearly evergreen where winters are fairly mild. This, too, is a substantial, rounded shrub, but only 12 to 20 feet in all directions. Its 6- to 8-inch springtime flower clusters look like big popcorn balls; the flowers are sterile, so no fruits are produced.

Two evergreen viburnums are hardy to 0°F/–18°C. For beauty of foliage, *V. davidii* is not surpassed: broad 6-inch-long ovals, glossy and dark green, characterized by prominent veins from base to tip. One plant makes a slowly spreading clump, the branches growing 2 to 3 feet high and spreading wider, carrying the elegant foliage to the ground. In spring, small clusters of white flowers appear at branch tips; metallic blue fruits follow if several plants grow together for pollination. This is an excellent shrub for mass planting, even as a small-scale ground cover.

Flowers and fruits are more of a feature in laurustinus, *V. tinus*. The basic species can reach 12 feet high and 6 feet wide, dense and upright, with glossy, 3-inch dark green leaves. New leaf stems are a distinctive wine red. From mid-autumn into the following spring, pink buds open to white flowers in 4-inch clusters. Blue fruits last all summer.

Among named selections of laurustinus, 'Variegatus' has leaves marked in white and cream, while 'Lucidum' and 'Robustum' have larger leaves. 'Spring Bouquet' has slightly smaller leaves on a compact plant 6 to 10 feet high; 'Dwarf' is shorter still, 3 to 5 feet, and rounded rather than upright. In any form, laurustinus is a first-rate choice in mild climates for use as an unclipped hedge or screen.

Culture. Adaptable and unfussy, these shrubs can grow well in hot and cool, humid and dry climates. Good soil encourages best growth, but acidity or mild alkalinity is not an issue; for best appearance, water routinely during dry periods.

Good companions. *Acer, Cercis, Cornus, Hamamelis, Rhododendron, Stewartia.*

❧

VIOLA

Violet
Deciduous and evergreen perennials
Hardy to –10°F/–23°C except as noted
Part to full shade/regular water

The legendary purple-flowered sweet violet *(V. odorata)* is just one of several similar species that will provide carpets of low foliage and a profusion of spring flowers. All have rounded leaves carried at the ends of slender leafstalks; flowers appear just above, and among, the leaves.

Evergreen *V. odorata* is one of the first flowers to announce the start of the spring floral parade—as early as late winter in milder regions. Plants are just 4 to 8 inches high, growing like strawberries by sending out runners that root and produce new plants. This makes sweet

violet a fine ground cover along pathways, under deciduous shrubs and trees, and among larger perennials. An established patch will remain a sheet of color for more than a month—exuding the justly famous fragrance. Purple is the classic color, but specialists carry kinds with flowers in light to dark blue, pink, lilac, and white.

A small group of *V. odorata* hybrids, the Parma violets, features double and powerfully fragrant blossoms on compact plants hardy to 10°F/–12°C. Colors range from deep violet through lavender and pink to white.

Deciduous Confederate violet, *V. sororia (V. priceana)*, makes clumps of thick rootstocks instead of spreading into colonies. But it will self-seed profusely if you don't remove spent flowers, thus assuring its spread. Spring blossoms resemble small pansies: white, heavily veined in blue.

Culture. Violets grow best in good soil into which plenty of organic matter has been incorporated. But they will grow fairly well in poorer, less humus-rich soil as long as they get supplemental water during dry periods.

Violets can take considerable sunshine early in the year while in flower, making them good candidates for planting under deciduous trees.

Good companions. *Aspidistra, Helleborus, Hosta, Polygonatum, Pulmonaria, Trillium.*

VIOLA odorata 'Freckles'

ENCYCLOPEDIA OF SHADE PLANTS

Index

All photographs and illustrations, except those in the encyclopedia, pages 58–110, are indicated by **boldface** page numbers.